Moral Luck

Philosophical Papers 1973–1980

Moral Luck

Philosophical Papers 1973–1980

BERNARD WILLIAMS

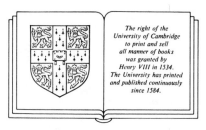

The right of the
University of Cambridge
to print and sell
all manner of books
was granted by
Henry VIII in 1534.
The University has printed
and published continuously
since 1584.

CAMBRIDGE UNIVERSITY PRESS
Cambridge
London   New York   New Rochelle
Melbourne   Sydney

Published by the Press Syndicate of the University of Cambridge
The Pitt Building, Trumpington Street, Cambridge CB2 1RP
32 East 57th Street, New York, NY 10022, USA
10 Stamford Road, Oakleigh, Melbourne 3166, Australia

First published 1981
Reprinted 1983, 1985, 1986

Printed in Great Britain by the
University Press, Cambridge

Library of Congress catalogue card number: 81–10152

British Library Cataloguing in Publication Data

Williams, Bernard
Moral luck: philosophical papers 1973–1980.
1. Philosophy
I. Title
192   B1674w/

ISBN 0 521 24372 6 hard covers
ISBN 0 521 28691 3 paperback

To Isaiah and Aline Berlin

Contents

Preface

The papers collected here have all been published in the past seven years, mostly in collective volumes, in three cases as contributions to *Festschriften*. I am grateful to editors and publishers for their agreement to republication. Most of the essays are substantially unchanged, though I have made some stylistic alteration to all of them. Three have undergone rather greater change. In the case of *Justice as a Virtue*, which was written for a volume on Aristotle's moral philosophy, the aim has been to take away some of the more detailed exegesis. The most extensive revisions have been to *Moral Luck* itself, where I have tried to get the main idea under rather better control than it was in the first version. I have not entirely succeeded, and in deciding to give its name to the book, my aim has been not to draw particular attention to that essay, but rather to suggest something which may indeed have contributed to its imperfections – that concerns echoed in that title are picked up in different forms in several parts of the book.

It will be obvious that certain worries both in and about moral philosophy, and also certain images of human action and practical thought, run through most of the papers. It is also obvious, when the papers are brought together, that they raise some pressing questions which they do not do much to answer. The ideas which occur here certainly need some rather more systematic framework, and I hope to be able to publish work in that direction in the course of the next few years. I do not think, however, that such a framework could have helpfully preceded these ideas – if there is anything in them, then they have to shape it.

Moral philosophy certainly needs the benefits of theory, but of theory in other parts of philosophy. I am more than ever convinced that what it does not need is a theory of its own. There cannot be any very interesting, tidy or self-contained theory of what morality is, nor, despite the vigorous activities of some present practitioners, can there be an ethical theory, in the sense of a philosophical structure which, together with some degree of empirical fact, will yield a decision procedure for moral reasoning. This latter undertaking has never succeeded, and could not succeed, in answering the question, *by what right* does it legislate to the moral sentiments? The abstract and schematic conceptions of 'rationality' which are usually deployed in this connection do not even look as though they were relevant to the question – so soon, at least, as morality is seen as something whose real existence must consist in personal experience and social institutions, not in sets of propositions.

One should rather say: any real existence that it may have. A further difficulty for these theoretical undertakings is something which is an historical truth, and therefore (by now) a philosophical problem, that morality itself is problematical, not merely in content, but in its supposed existence as a dimension of practical thought or social evaluation at all. The fact that the words 'moral' or 'morality' occur in the titles of no less than five of the present essays should be taken as signalling a widening doubt, rather than a simple territorial acknowledgement. It is this doubt, as well as scepticism about the powers of moral or ethical theory, which has led me to try to find out – often by the crude method of prodding it – which parts of moral thought seemed to me to be actually alive, before trying to design any elegant physiology for it.

The last two essays stand apart from the rest, even if there is some link through the piece on Relativism. They are reprinted for any independent interest they may have, but there are in fact preoccupations that relate them to the rest. They both raise the question of the extent to which we can hope to attain to any conception of the world which will be independent of our peculiarities and the peculiarities of our perspective – an aim which has been that of many philosophers, and remains that of almost all scientists. The question of the extent to which such a representation of the world may be possible is intimately connected with issues in moral philosophy. It is a question central to the definition of scientific discovery, and that notion – which seems to have been left high and dry by the most sceptical treatments of this problem in recent philosophy – still provides a central contrast with changes in moral understanding, despite a very welcome decline in interest in a blank contrast of 'fact' and 'value'. At the same time, the perspectiveless or 'absolute' view of things which has been an ambition for science has a certain analogue in the external view of action and experience which, on many views of the matter, is called for by moral impartiality – what Sidgwick, in a memorably absurd phrase, called 'the point of view of the universe'. These models, for scientific enquiry and for morality, lay similar claims to expressing an idea of objectivity. To assess those claims and to compare them remains a central and pressing demand on philosophy.

B.W.

Cambridge, March 1981

Acknowledgements

These papers originally appeared in the places listed below. Permission from the publishers to reprint them is gratefully acknowledged.

'Persons, character and morality' in A. O. Rorty (ed.), *The identities of persons* (Berkeley: University of California Press, 1976); 'Moral luck', *Proceedings of the Aristotelian Society*, supplementary volume L (1976), 115–35; 'Utilitarianism and moral self-indulgence' in H. D. Lewis (ed.), *Contemporary British Philosophy, personal statements*, fourth series (London: Allen and Unwin, 1976); 'Politics and moral character' in Stuart Hampshire (ed.), *Public and private morality* (Cambridge: Cambridge University Press, 1978); 'Conflicts of values' in Alan Ryan (ed.), *The idea of freedom: essays in honour of Isaiah Berlin* (Oxford: Oxford University Press, 1979); 'Justice as a virtue' in A. O. Rorty, *Essays on Aristotle's Ethics* (Berkeley: University of California Press, 1981); 'Rawls and Pascal's wager', *Cambridge Review* (Feb. 1975); 'Internal and external reasons' in Ross Harrison (ed.), *Rational action* (Cambridge: Cambridge University Press, 1980); '*Ought* and moral obligation': rewritten from 'Moral obligation and the semantics of *ought*' in E. Morscher and R. Stranzinger (eds.) *Proceedings of the Fifth Kirchberg Wittgenstein Symposium 1980* (forthcoming); 'Practical necessity' in Brian Hebblethwaite and Stewart Sutherland (eds.), *The philosophical frontiers of Christian theology: essays presented to D. M. MacKinnon* (Cambridge: Cambridge University Press, 1982); 'The truth in relativism', *Proceedings of the Aristotelian Society*, volume LXXV (1974–75) 215–28; 'Wittgenstein and idealism' in Godfrey Vesey (ed.), *Understanding Wittgenstein*, Royal Institute of Philosophy Lectures, volume seven 1972–1973 (London: Macmillan, 1974); 'Another time, another place, another person' in G. F. Macdonald (ed.), *Perception and identity: essays presented to A. J. Ayer with his replies to them* (London: Macmillan, 1979).

1 Persons, character and morality

Much of the most interesting recent work in moral philosophy has been
of basically Kantian inspiration; Rawls' own work[1] and those to
varying degrees influenced by him such as Richards[2] and Nagel[3] are
very evidently in the debt of Kant, while it is interesting that a writer
such as Fried[4] who gives evident signs of being pulled away from some
characteristic features of this way of looking at morality nevertheless,
I shall suggest later, tends to get pulled back into it. This is not of course
a very pure Kantianism, and still less is it an expository or subservient
one. It differs from Kant among other things in making no demands
on a theory of noumenal freedom, and also, importantly, in admitting
considerations of a general empirical character in determining fundamental moral demands, which Kant at least supposed himself not to
be doing. But allowing for those and many other important differences,
the inspiration is there and the similarities both significant and
acknowledged. They extend far beyond the evident point that both
the extent and the nature of opposition to Utilitarianism resembles
Kant's: though it is interesting that in this respect they are more Kantian
than a philosophy which bears an obvious but superficial formal
resemblance to Kantianism, namely Hare's. Indeed, Hare now supposes
that when a substantial moral theory is elicited from his philosophical
premises, it turns out to be a version of Utilitarianism. This is not
merely because the universal and prescriptive character of moral
judgements lays on the agent, according to Hare, a requirement of
hypothetical identification with each person affected by a given

---

[1] John Rawls, *A Theory of Justice* (Oxford, 1972).
[2] D. A. J. Richards, *A Theory of Reasons for Action* (Oxford, 1971).
[3] Thomas Nagel, *The Possibility of Altruism* (Oxford, 1970).
[4] Charles Fried, *An Anatomy of Values* (Cambridge, Mass., 1970).

decision – so much is a purely Kantian element. It is rather that each identification is treated just as yielding 'acceptance' or 'rejection' of a certain prescription, and they in turn are construed solely in terms of satisfactions, so that the outputs of the various identifications can, under the usual Utilitarian assumptions, be regarded additively.

Among Kantian elements in these outlooks are, in particular, these: that the moral point of view is basically different from a non-moral, and in particular self-interested, point of view, and by a difference of kind; that the moral point of view is specially characterized by its impartiality and its indifference to any particular relations to particular persons, and that moral thought requires abstraction from particular circumstances and particular characteristics of the parties, including the agent, except in so far as these can be treated as universal features of any morally similar situation; and that the motivations of a moral agent, correspondingly, involve a rational application of impartial principle and are thus different in kind from the sorts of motivations that he might have for treating some particular persons (for instance, though not exclusively, himself) differently because he happened to have some particular interest towards them. Of course, it is not intended that these demands should exclude other and more intimate relations nor prevent someone from acting in ways demanded by and appropriate to them: that is a matter of the relations of the moral point of view to other points of view. But I think it is fair to say that included among the similarities of these views to Kant's is the point that like his they do not make the question of the relations between those points of view at all easy to answer. The deeply disparate character of moral and of non-moral motivation, together with the special dignity or supremacy attached to the moral, make it very difficult to assign to those other relations and motivations the significance or structural importance in life which some of them are capable of possessing.

It is worth remarking that this detachment of moral motivations and the moral point of view from the level of particular relations to particular persons, and more generally from the level of all motivations and perceptions other than those of an impartial character, obtains even when the moral point of view is itself explained in terms of the self-interest under conditions of ignorance of some abstractly conceived contracting parties, as it is by Rawls, and by Richards, who is particularly concerned with applying directly to the characterization of the moral interest, the structure used by Rawls chiefly to characterize social justice. For while the contracting parties are pictured as making some kind of self-interested or prudential choice of a set of rules, they are entirely abstract persons making this choice in ignorance of their own particular properties, tastes, and so forth; and the self-interested choice of an abstract agent is intended to model precisely the moral choice of a concrete agent, by representing what he would choose granted that he made just the kinds of abstraction from his actual personality, situation and relations which the Kantian picture of moral experience requires.

Some elements in this very general picture serve already to distinguish the outlook in question from Utilitarianism. Choices made in deliberate abstraction from empirical information which actually exists are necessarily from a Utilitarian point of view irrational, and to that extent the formal structure of the outlook, even allowing the admission of *general* empirical information, is counter-Utilitarian. There is a further point of difference with Utilitarianism, which comes out if one starts from the fact that there is one respect at least in which Utilitarianism itself requires a notable abstraction in moral thought, an abstraction which in this respect goes even further than the Kantians': if Kantianism abstracts in moral thought from the identity of persons, Utilitarianism strikingly abstracts from their separateness. This is true in more than one way. First, as the Kantian theorists have themselves emphasized, persons lose their separateness as beneficiaries of the Utilitarian provisions, since in the form which maximizes total utility, and even in that which maximizes average utility, there is an agglomeration of satisfactions which is basically indifferent to the separateness of those who have the satisfactions; this is evidently so in the total maximization system, and it is only superficially not so in the average maximization system, where the agglomeration occurs before the division. Richards,[5] following Rawls, has suggested that the device of the ideal observer serves to model the agglomeration of these satisfactions: equivalent to the world could be one person, with an indefinite capacity for happiness and pain. The Kantian view stands opposed to this; the idea of the contractual element, even between these shadowy and abstract participants, is in part to make the point that

[5] Richards, op. cit., p. 87 al; cf. Rawls, op. cit., p. 27; also Nagel, op. cit., p. 134. This is not the only, nor perhaps historically the soundest, interpretation of the device: cf. Derek Parfit, 'Later Selves and Moral Principles', in A. Montefiore, ed., *Philosophy and Personal Relations* (London, 1973), pp. 149–50 and nn. 30–4.

there are limitations built in at the bottom to permissible trade-offs between the satisfactions of individuals.

A second aspect of the Utilitarian abstraction from separateness involves agency.[6] It turns on the point that the basic bearer of value for Utilitarianism is the *state of affairs*, and hence, when the relevant causal differences have been allowed for, it cannot make any further difference who produces a given state of affairs: if S1 consists of my doing something, together with consequences, and S2 consists of someone else doing something, with consequences, and S2 comes about just in case S1 does not, and S1 is better than S2, then I should bring about S1, however *prima facie* nasty S1 is. Thus, unsurprisingly, the doctrine of negative responsibility has its roots at the foundation of Utilitarianism; and whatever projects, desires, ideals, or whatever I may have as a particular individual, as a Utilitarian agent my action has to be the output of *all* relevant causal items bearing on the situation, including all projects and desires within causal reach, my own and others. As a Utilitarian agent, I am just the representative of the satisfaction system who happens to be near certain causal levers at a certain time. At this level, there is abstraction not merely from the identity of agents, but, once more, from their separateness, since a conceivable extension or restriction of the causal powers of a given agent could always replace the activities of some other agent, so far as Utilitarian outcomes are concerned, and an outcome allocated to two agents as things are could equivalently be the product of one agent, or three, under a conceivable redistribution of causal powers.

In this latter respect also the Kantian outlook can be expected to disagree. For since we are concerned not just with outcomes, but at a basic level with actions and policies, *who* acts in a given situation makes a difference, and in particular I have a particular responsibility for *my* actions. Thus in more than one way the Kantian outlook emphasizes something like the separateness of agents, and in that sense makes less of an abstraction than Utilitarianism does (though, as we have seen, there are other respects, with regard to causally relevant empirical facts, in which its abstraction is greater). But now the question arises, of whether the honourable instincts of Kantianism to defend the individuality of individuals against the agglomerative indifference of Utilitarianism can in fact be effective granted the impoverished and abstract character of persons as moral agents which

---

[6] For a more detailed account, see 'A Critique of Utilitarianism', in J. J. C. Smart and B. Williams, *Utilitarianism: For and Against* (Cambridge, 1973).

the Kantian view seems to impose. Findlay has said 'the separateness
of persons...is...the basic fact for morals',[7] and Richards hopes to
have respected that fact.[8] Similarly Rawls claims that impartiality does
not mean impersonality.[9] But it is a real question, whether the
conception of the individual provided by the Kantian theories is in fact
enough to yield what is wanted, even by the Kantians; let alone enough
for others who, while equally rejecting Utilitarianism, want to allow
more room than Kantianism can allow for the importance of individual
character and personal relations in moral experience.

i.e. individuals as moral agents

II

I am going to take up two aspects of this large subject. They both
involve the idea that an individual person has a set of desires, concerns
or, as I shall often call them, projects, which help to constitute a
character. The first issue concerns the connection between that fact and
the man's having a reason for living at all. I approach this through
a discussion of some work by Derek Parfit; though I touch on a variety
of points in this, my overriding aim is to emphasize the basic
importance for our thought of the ordinary idea of a self or person
which undergoes changes of character, as opposed to an approach
which, even if only metaphorically, would dissolve the person, under
changes of character, into a series of 'selves'.

In this section I am concerned just with the point that each person
has a character, not with the point that different people have different
characters. That latter point comes more to the fore on the second issue,
which I take up in part III, and which concerns personal relations. Both
issues suggest that the Kantian view contains an important
misrepresentation.

First, then, I should like to comment on some arguments of Parfit
which explore connections between moral issues and a certain view
of personal identity: a view which, he thinks, might offer, among other
things, '*some* defence'[10] of the Utilitarian neglect of the separateness
of persons. This view Parfit calls the 'Complex View'. This view takes
seriously the idea that relations of psychological connectedness (such
as memory and persistence of character and motivation) are what really

---

[7] Findlay, *Values and Intentions* (London, 1961), pp. 235–6.
[8] Richards, op. cit., p. 87.   [9] Rawls, op. cit., p. 190.
[10] Parfit, op. cit., p. 160, his emphasis. In what follows and elsewhere in this chapter
I am grateful to Parfit for valuable criticisms of an earlier draft.

matter with regard to most questions which have been discussed in relation to personal identity. The suggestion is that morality should take this seriously as well, and that there is more than one way of its doing so. Psychological connectedness (unlike the surface logic of personal identity) admits of degrees. Let us call the relevant properties and relations which admit of degrees, *scalar* items. One of Parfit's aims is to make moral thought reflect more directly the scalar character of phenomena which underlie personal identity. In particular, in those cases in which the scalar relations hold in reduced degree, this fact should receive recognition in moral thought.

Another, and more general, consequence of taking the Complex View is that the matter of personal identity may appear altogether less deep, as Parfit puts it, than if one takes the Simple View, as he calls that alternative view which sees as basically significant the all-or-nothing logic of personal identity. If the matter of personal identity appears less deep, the *separateness* of persons, also, may come to seem less an ultimate and specially significant consideration for morality. The connection between those two thoughts is not direct, but there is more than one indirect connection between them.[11]

So far as the problems of *agency* are concerned, Parfit's treatment is not going to help Utilitarianism. His loosening of identity is diachronic, by reference to the weakening of psychological connectedness over time: where there is such weakening to a sufficient degree, he is prepared to speak of 'successive selves', though this is intended only as a *façon de parler*.[12] But the problems that face Utilitarianism about agency can arise with any agent whose projects stretch over enough time, and are sufficiently grounded in character, to be in any substantial sense *his* projects, and that condition will be satisfied by something that is, for Parfit, even *one* self. Thus there is nothing in this degree of dissolution of the traditional self which can help over agency.

In discussing the issues involved in making moral thought reflect more directly the scalar nature of what underlies personal identity, it is important to keep in mind that the talk of 'past selves', 'future selves' and generally 'several selves' is only a convenient fiction. Neglect of this may make the transpositions in moral thought required by the

---

[11] Parfit develops one such connection in the matter of distributive justice: pp. 148ff. In general it can be said that one very natural correlate of being impressed by the separateness of several persons' lives is being impressed by the peculiar unity of one person's life.   [12] Ibid., n. 14, pp. 161–2.

Complex View seem simpler and perhaps more inviting than they are, since they may glide along on what seems to be a mere multiplication, in the case of these new 'selves', of familiar interpersonal relations. We must concentrate on the scalar facts. But many moral notions show a notable resistance to reflecting the scalar: or, rather, to reflecting it in the right way. We may take the case of promising, which Parfit has discussed.[13] Suppose that I promise to A that I will help him in certain ways in three years time. In three years time a person appears, let us say $A^\star$, whose memories, character etc., bear some, but a rather low, degree of connectedness to A's. How am I to mirror these scalar facts in my thought about whether, or how, I am to carry out my promise?

Something, first, should be said about the promise itself. '*You*' was the expression it used: 'I will help *you*', and it used that expression in such a way that it covered both the recipient of these words and the potential recipient of the help. This was not a promise that could be carried out (or, more generally, honoured) by helping anyone else, or indeed by doing anything except helping that person I addressed when I said 'you' – thus the situation is not like that with some promises to the dead (those where there is still something one can do about it).[14] If there is to be any action of mine which is to count as honouring that promise, it will have to be action which consists in now helping $A^\star$. How am I to mirror, in my action and my thought about it, $A^\star$'s scalar relations to A?

There seem to be only three ways in which they could be so mirrored, and none seems satisfactory. First, the action promised might itself have some significant scalar dimension, and it might be suggested that this should vary with my sense of the proximity or remoteness of $A^\star$ from A. But this will not do: it is clearly a lunatic idea that if I promised to pay A a sum of money, then my obligation is to pay $A^\star$ some money, but a smaller sum. A more serious suggestion would be that what varies with the degree of connectedness of $A^\star$ to A is the degree of stringency of the obligation to do what was promised. While less evidently dotty, it is still, on reflection, dotty; thus, to take a perhaps unfair example, it seems hard to believe that if someone had promised to marry A, they would have an obligation to marry $A^\star$, only an obligation which came lower down the queue.

What, in contrast, is an entirely familiar sort of thought is, last of all, one that embodies degrees of doubt or obscurity whether a given

[13] Ibid., pp. 144ff.   [14] Ibid., p. 144 fin.

obligation (of fixed stringency) applies or not. Thus a secret agent might think that he was obliged to kill the man in front of him if and only if that man was Martin Bormann; and be in doubt whether he should kill this man, because he was in doubt whether it was Bormann. (Contrast the two analogously dotty types of solution to this case: that, at any rate, he is obliged to wound him; or, that he is obliged to kill him, but it has a lower priority than it would have otherwise.) But this type of thought is familiar at the cost of not really embodying the scalar facts; it is a style of thought appropriate to uncertainty about a matter of all-or-nothing and so embodies in effect what Parfit calls the Simple View, that which does not take seriously the scalar facts to which the Complex View addresses itself.

These considerations do not, of course show that there are no ways of mirroring the Complex View in these areas of moral thought, but they do suggest that the displacements required are fairly radical. It is significant that by far the easiest place in which to find the influence of the scalar considerations is in certain *sentiments*, which themselves have a scalar dimension – here we can see a place where the Complex View and Utilitarianism easily fit together. But the structure of such sentiments is not adequate to produce the structure of all moral thought. The rest of it will have to be more radically adapted, or abandoned, if the Complex View is really to have its effect.

One vitally important item which is in part (though only in part) scalar is a man's concern for (what commonsense would call) his own future. That a man should have some interest now in what he will do or undergo later, requires that he have some desires or projects or concerns now which relate to those doings or happenings later; or, as a special case of that, that some very general desire or project or concern of his now relate to desires or projects which he will have then. The limiting case, at the basic physical level, is that in which he is merely concerned with future pain, and it may be that that concern can properly reach through any degree of psychological discontinuity.[15] But even if so, it is not our present concern, since the mere desire to avoid physical pain is not adequate to constitute a character. We are here concerned with more distinctive and structured patterns of desire and project, and there are possible psychological changes in these which could be predicted for a person and which would put his future after such changes beyond his present interest. Such a future would be, so to speak, over the horizon of his interest, though of course if the future

[15] Cf. 'The Self and the Future', in *Problems of the Self* (Cambridge, 1973).

picture could be filled in as a *series* of changes leading from here to there, he might recapture an interest in the outcome.

In this connection, to take the language of 'future selves' at all literally would be deeply misleading: it would be to take the same facts twice over. My concern for my descendants or other relatives may be, as Parfit says, to some degree proportional to their remoteness from me; equally, my concern for other persons in general can vary with the degree to which their character is congenial to my own, their projects sympathetic to my outlook. The two considerations, of proximity and congeniality, evidently interact – ways in which they can reinforce or cancel one another are, for instance, among the commonplaces of dynastic fiction. But the proximity of Parfitian 'later selves' to me, their ancestor, just consists of the relations of their character and interests to my present ones. I cannot first identify a later self 'descendant', and then consider the relations of his character to mine, since it is just the presence or lack of these relations which in good part determines his proximity and even his existence as a separate self.

Thus if I take steps now to hinder what will or may predictably be my future projects, as in Parfit's Russian nobleman case,[16] it would be a case of double vision to see this as my treating my future self as another person, since, spelled out, that would have to mean, treating my future self as another person *of whose projects I disapprove*; and therein lies the double vision. To insist here that what I would be doing is to hinder *my own* future projects (where it is understood that that is not necessarily a foolish thing to do) is to keep hold on a number of deeply important facts. One is that to contemplate, or expect, or regard as probable, such changes in my own character is different from my relation to them in someone else (still more, of course, from my attitude to the mere *arrival* of someone else with a different character). The question must arise, how prediction is, in my own case, related to acquiescence, and special and obscure issues arise about the range of methods that it could be appropriate or rational for a man to use to prevent or deflect predicted changes in his own character. Thought about those issues must take as basic the *he* for whom these changes would be changes in *his* character.

Relatedly, there is the question of why I should regard my present projects and outlook as having more authority than my future ones. I do *not* mean by that the question, why I should not distribute consideration equally over my whole life: I shall later touch on the

[16] Parfit, op. cit., pp. 145ff.

point that it is a mistake of Kantians (and perhaps of some kinds of Utilitarians too) to think it *a priori* evident that one rationally should do that. I mean rather the question of how, in the supposed type of example, I evaluate the two successive outlooks. Why should I hinder my future projects from the perspective of my present values rather than inhibit my present projects from the perspective of my future values? It is not enough in answer to that to say that evidently present action must flow from present values. If the future prospect were of something now identified as a growth in enlightenment, present action would try to hinder present projects in its interest. For that to be so, there indeed would have to be now some dissatisfaction with one's present values, but that consideration just turns attention, in the Russian nobleman case, to the corresponding question, of why the young man is so unquestioningly satisfied with his present values. He may have, for instance, a theory of degeneration of the middle-aged, but then he should reflect that, when middle-aged, he will have a theory of the naiveté of the young.

I am not saying that there are no answers to any of these questions, or that there is no way out of this kind of diachronic relativism. The point is that if it is true that this man will change in these ways, it is only by understanding his present projects *as the projects of one who will so change* that he can understand them even as his present projects; and if he knows that he will so change, then it is only through such an understanding that he could justifiably give his present values enough authority to defeat his future values, as he clear-headedly conceives them to be. If he clear-headedly knows that his present projects are solely the projects of his youth, how does he know that they are not *merely* that, unless he has some view which makes sense of, among other things, his own future? One cannot even start on the important questions of how this man, so totally identified with his present values, will be related to his future without them, if one does not take as basic the fact that it is his own future that he will be living through without them.

This leads to the question of why we go on at all.

It might be wondered why, unless we believe in a possibly hostile after-life, or else are in a muddle which the Epicureans claimed to expose, we should regard death as an evil.[17] One answer to that is that we desire certain things; if one desires something, then to that extent one has reason to resist the happening of anything which

[17] The argument is developed in more detail in *Problems of the Self*, pp. 82ff.

prevents one getting it, and death certainly does that, for a large range of desires. Some desires are admittedly contingent on the prospect of one's being alive, but not all desires can be in that sense conditional, since it is possible to imagine a person rationally contemplating suicide, in the face of some predicted evil, and if he decides to go on in life, then he is propelled forward into it by some desire (however general or inchoate) which cannot operate conditionally on his being alive, since it settles the question of whether he is going to be alive. Such a desire we may call a *categorical* desire. Most people have many categorical desires, which do not depend on the assumption of the person's existence, since they serve to prevent that assumption's being questioned, or to answer the question if it is raised. Thus one's pattern of interests, desires and projects not only provide the reason for an interest in what happens within the horizon of one's future, but also constitute the conditions of there being such a future at all.

Here, once more, to deal in terms of later selves who were like descendants would be to misplace the heart of the problem. Whether to commit suicide, and whether to leave descendants, are two separate decisions: one can produce children before committing suicide. A person might even choose deliberately to do that, for comprehensible sorts of reasons; or again one could be deterred, as by the thought that one would not be there to look after them. Later selves, however, evade all these thoughts by having the strange property that while they come into existence only with the death of their ancestor, the physical death of their ancestor will abort them entirely. The analogy seems unhelpfully strained, when we are forced to the conclusion that the failure of all my projects, and my consequent suicide, would take with me all my 'descendants', although they are in any case a kind of descendants who arise only with my ceasing to exist. More than unhelpfully, it runs together what are two quite different questions: whether, my projects having failed, I should cease to exist, and whether I shall have descendants whose projects may be quite different from mine and are in any case largely unknown. The analogy makes every question of the first kind involve a question of the second kind, and thus obscures the peculiar significance of the first question to the theory of the self. If, on the other hand, a man's future self is not another self, but the future of his self, then it is unproblematic why it should be eliminated with the failure of that which might propel him into it. The primacy of one's ordinary self is given, once more, by the thought that it is precisely what will not be in the world if one commits suicide.

The language of 'later selves', too literally taken, could exaggerate in one direction the degree to which my relation to some of my own projects resembles my relation to the projects of others. The Kantian emphasis on moral impartiality exaggerates it in quite another, by providing ultimately too slim a sense in which any projects are mine at all. This point once more involves the idea that my present projects are the condition of my existence,[18] in the sense that unless I am propelled forward by the conatus of desire, project and interest, it is unclear why I should go on at all: the world, certainly, as a kingdom of moral agents, has no particular claim on my presence or, indeed, interest in it. (That kingdom, like others, has to respect the natural right to emigration.) Now the categorical desires which propel one on do not have to be even very evident to consciousness, let alone grand or large; one good testimony to one's existence having a point is that the question of its point does not arise, and the propelling concerns may be of a relatively everyday kind such as certainly provide the ground of many sorts of happiness. Equally, while these projects may present *some* conflicts with the demands of morality, as Kantianly conceived, these conflicts may be fairly minor; after all – and I do not want to deny or forget it – these projects, in a normally socialized individual, have in good part been formed within, and formed by, dispositions which constitute a commitment to morality. But, on the other hand, the possibility of radical conflict is also there. A man may have, for a lot of his life or even just for some part of it, a *ground* project or set of projects which are closely related to his existence and which to a significant degree give a meaning to his life.

I do not mean by that they provide him with a life-plan, in Rawls' sense. On the contrary, Rawls' conception, and the conception of practical rationality, shared by Nagel, which goes with it, seems to me rather to imply an external view of one's own life, as something like a given rectangle that has to be optimally filled in.[19] This perspective

---

[18] We can note the consequence that present projects are the condition of future ones. This view stands in opposition to Nagel's: as do the formulations used above, p. 10. But while, as Nagel says, taking a rational interest in preparing for the realization of my later projects does not require that they be my present projects, it seems nevertheless true that it presupposes my having some present projects which directly or indirectly reach out to a time when those later projects will be my projects.

[19] It is of course a separate question what the criteria of optimality are, but it is not surprising that a view which presupposes that no risks are taken with the useful area

omits the vital consideration already mentioned, that the continuation and size of this rectangle is up to me; so, slightly less drastically, is the question of how much of it I care to cultivate. The correct perspective on one's life is *from now*. The consequences of that for practical reasoning (particularly with regard to the relevance of proximity or remoteness in time of one's objective), is a large question which cannot be pursued here; here we need only the idea of a man's ground projects providing the motive force which propels him into the future, and gives him a reason for living.

For a project to play this ground role, it does not have to be true that if it were frustrated or in any of various ways he lost it, he would have to commit suicide, nor does he have to think that. Other things, or the mere hope of other things, may keep him going. But he may feel in those circumstances that he might as well have died. Of course, in general a man does not have one separable project which plays this ground role: rather, there is a nexus of projects, related to his conditions of life, and it would be the loss of all or most of them that would remove meaning.

Ground projects do not have to be selfish, in the sense that they are just concerned with things for the agent. Nor do they have to be self-centred, in the sense that the creative projects of a Romantic artist could be considered self-centred (where it has to be *him*, but not *for* him). They may certainly be altruistic, and in a very evident sense moral, projects; thus he may be working for reform, or justice, or general improvement. There is no contradiction in the idea of a man's dying for a ground project – quite the reverse, since if death really is necessary for the project, then to live would be to live with it unsatisfied, something which, if it really is his ground project, he has no reason to do.

That a man's projects were altruistic or moral would not make them immune to conflict with impartial morality, any more than the artist's projects are immune. Admittedly *some* conflicts are ruled out by the projects sincerely being *those* projects; thus a man devoted to the cause of curing injustice in a certain place, cannot just insist on his plan for doing that over others', if convinced that theirs will be as effective as

of the rectangle should also favour a very low risk strategy in filling it: cf. Rawls (on prudential rationality in general), op. cit., p. 422: 'we have the guiding principle that a rational individual is always to act so that he need never blame himself no matter how things finally transpire.' Cf. also the passages cited in Rawls' footnote. For more on this and the relations of ground projects to rationality, see chapter 2, below.

his (something it may be hard to convince him of). For if he does insist on that, then we learn that his concern is not merely that injustice be removed, but that *he* remove it – not necessarily a dishonourable concern, but a different one. Thus some conflicts are ruled out by the project being not self-centred. But not all conflicts: thus his selfless concern for justice may do havoc to quite other commitments.

A man who has such a ground project will be required by Utilitarianism to give up what it requires in a given case just if that conflicts with what he is required to do as an impersonal utility-maximizer when all the causally relevant considerations are in. That is a quite absurd requirement.[20] But the Kantian, who can do rather better than that, still cannot do well enough. For impartial morality, if the conflict really does arise, must be required to win; and that cannot necessarily be a reasonable demand on the agent. There can come a point at which it is quite unreasonable for a man to give up, in the name of the impartial good ordering of the world of moral agents, something which is a condition of his having any interest in being around in that world at all. Once one thinks about what is involved in having a character, one can see that the Kantians' omission of character is a condition of their ultimate insistence on the demands of impartial morality, just as it is a reason for finding inadequate their account of the individual.

III

All this argument depends on the idea of one person's having a character, in the sense of having projects and categorical desires with which that person is identified; nothing has yet been said about different persons having different characters. It is perhaps important, in order to avoid misunderstanding, to make clear a way in which difference of character does *not* come into the previous argument. It does not come in by way of the man's thinking that only if he affirms these projects will they be affirmed, while (by contrast) the aims of Kantian morality can be affirmed by anyone. Though that thought could be present in some cases, it is not the point of the argument. The man is not pictured as thinking that he will have earned his place in the world, if his project is affirmed: that a distinctive contribution to the world will have been made, if his distinctive project is carried forward. The point is that he wants these things, finds his life bound

[20] Cf. 'A Critique of Utilitarianism', sections 3–5.

up with them, and that they propel him forward, and thus they give
him a reason for living his life. But that is compatible with these drives,
and this life, being much like others'. They give him, distinctively, a
reason for living this life, in the sense that he has no desire to give
up and make room for others, but they do not require him to lead
a *distinctive* life. While this is so, and the point has some importance,
nevertheless the interest and substance of most of the discussion
depends on its in fact being the case that people have dissimilar
characters and projects. Our *general* view of these matters, and the
significance given to individuality in our own and others' lives, would
certainly change if there were not between persons indefinitely many
differences which are important to us. The level of description is of
course also vital for determining what is the same or different. A similar
description can be given of two people's dispositions, but the concrete
detail be perceived very differently – and it is a feature of our
experience of persons that we can perceive and be conscious of an
indefinitely fine degree of difference in concrete detail (though it is only
in certain connections and certain cultures that one spends much time
rehearsing it).

One area in which *difference* of character directly plays a role in the
concept of moral individuality is that of personal relations, and I shall
close with some remarks in this connection. Differences of character
give substance to the idea that individuals are not inter-substitutable.
As I have just argued, a particular man so long as he is propelled
forward does not need to assure himself that he is unlike others, in
order not to feel substitutable, but in his personal relations to others
the idea of difference can certainly make a contribution, in more than
one way. To the thought that his friend cannot just be equivalently
replaced by another friend, is added both the thought that he cannot
just be replaced himself, and also the thought that he and his friend
are different from each other. This last thought is important to us as
part of our view of friendship, a view thus set apart from Aristotle's
opinion that a good man's friend was a duplication of himself. This I
suspect to have been an Aristotelian, and not generally a Greek,
opinion. It is connected with another feature of his views which seems
even stranger to us, at least with regard to any deeply committed
friendship, namely that friendship for him has to be minimally
risky – one of his problems is indeed to reconcile the role of friendship
with his unappetizing ideal of self-sufficiency. Once one agrees that
a three-dimensional mirror would not represent the ideal of friendship,

one can begin to see both how some degree of difference can play an essential role, and, also, how a commitment or involvement with a particular other person might be one of the kinds of project which figured basically in a man's life in the ways already sketched – something which would be mysterious or even sinister on an Aristotelian account.

For Kantians, personal relations at least presuppose moral relations, and some are rather disposed to go further and regard them as a *species* of moral relations, as in the richly moralistic account given by Richards[21] of one of the four main principles of supererogation which would be accepted in 'the Original Position' (that is to say, adopted as a moral limitation):

a principle of mutual love requiring that people should not show personal affection and love to others on the basis of arbitrary physical characteristics alone, but rather on the basis of traits of personality and character related to acting on moral principles.

This righteous absurdity is no doubt to be traced to a feeling that love, even love based on 'arbitrary physical characteristics', is something which has enough power and even authority to conflict badly with morality unless it can be brought within it from the beginning, and evidently that is a sound feeling, though it is an optimistic Kantian who thinks that much will be done about that by the adoption of this principle in the Original Position. The weaker view, that love and similar relations presuppose moral relations, in the sense that one could love someone only if one also had to them the moral relations one has to all people, is less absurd, but also wrong. It is of course true that loving someone involves some relations of the kind that morality requires or imports more generally, but it does not follow from that that one cannot have them in a particular case unless one has them generally in the way the moral person does. Someone might be concerned about the interests of someone else, and even about carrying out promises he made to that person, while not very concerned about these things with other persons. To the extent (whatever it may be) that loving someone involves showing some of the same concerns in relation to them that the moral person shows, or at least thinks he ought to show, elsewhere, the lover's relations will be examples of moral relations, or at least resemble them, but this does not have to be because they are *applications to this case* of relations which the lover, *qua* moral person, more generally enters into. (That might not be the best

[21] Richards, op. cit., p. 94.

description of the situation even if he *is* a moral person who enters into such relations more generally.)

However, once morality is there, and also personal relations to be taken seriously, so is the possibility of conflict. This of course does not mean that if there is some friendship with which his life is much involved, then a man must prefer any possible demand of that over other, impartial, moral demands. That would be absurd, and also a pathological kind of friendship, since both parties exist in the world and it is part of the sense of their friendship that it exists in the world. But the possibility of conflict with substantial moral claims of others is there, and it is not only in the outcome. There can also be conflict with moral demands on how the outcome is arrived at: the situation may not have been subjected to an impartial process of resolution, and this fact itself may cause unease to the impartial moral consciousness. There is an example of such unease in a passage by Fried. After an illuminating discussion of the question why, if at all, we should give priority of resources to actual and present sufferers over absent or future ones, he writes:[22]

surely it would be absurd to insist that if a man could, at no risk or cost to himself, save one of two persons in equal peril, and one of those in peril was, say, his wife, he must treat both equally, perhaps by flipping a coin. One answer is that where the potential rescuer occupies no office such as that of captain of a ship, public health official or the like, the occurrence of the accident may itself stand as a sufficient randomizing event to meet the dictates of fairness, so he may prefer his friend, or loved one. Where the rescuer does occupy an official position, the argument that he must overlook personal ties is not unacceptable.

The most striking feature of this passage is the direction in which Fried implicitly places the onus of proof: the fact that coin-flipping would be inappropriate raises some question to which an 'answer' is required, while the resolution of the question by the rescuer's occupying an official position is met with what sounds like relief (though it remains unclear what that rescuer does when he 'overlooks personal ties' – does *he* flip a coin?). The thought here seems to be that it is unfair to the second victim that, the first being the rescuer's wife, they never even get a chance of being rescued; and the answer

---

[22] Fried, op. cit., p. 227. [Note 1981] Fried has perhaps now modified the view criticised here. He has himself used the idea of friendship as creating special moral relations, but in a connexion where, it seems to me, it is out of place: for criticism, see chapter 4, below.

(as I read the reference to the 'sufficient randomizing event') is that at another level it is sufficiently fair – although in this disaster this rescuer has a special reason for saving the other person, it might have been another disaster in which another rescuer had a special reason for saving them. But, apart from anything else, that 'might have been' is far too slim to sustain a reintroduction of the notion of fairness. The 'random' element in such events, as in certain events of tragedy, should be seen not so much as affording a justification, in terms of an appropriate application of a lottery, as being a reminder that some situations lie beyond justifications.

But has anything yet shown that? For even if we leave behind thoughts of higher-order randomization, surely *this* is a justification on behalf of the rescuer, that the person he chose to rescue was his wife? It depends on how much weight is carried by 'justification': the consideration that it was his wife is certainly, for instance, an explanation which should silence comment. But something more ambitious than this is usually intended, essentially involving the idea that moral principle can legitimate his preference, yielding the conclusion that in situations of this kind it is at least all right (morally permissible) to save one's wife. (This could be combined with a variety of higher-order thoughts to give it a rationale; rule-Utilitarians might favour the idea that in matters of this kind it is best for each to look after his own, like house insurance.) But this construction provides the agent with one thought too many: it might have been hoped by some (for instance, by his wife) that his motivating thought, fully spelled out, would be the thought that it was his wife, not that it was his wife and that in situations of this kind it is permissible to save one's wife.

Perhaps others will have other feelings about this case. But the point is that somewhere (and if not in this case, where?) one reaches the necessity that such things as deep attachments to other persons will express themselves in the world in ways which cannot at the same time embody the impartial view, and that they also run the risk of offending against it.

They run that risk if they exist at all; yet unless such things exist, there will not be enough substance or conviction in a man's life to compel his allegiance to life itself. Life has to have substance if anything is to have sense, including adherence to the impartial system; but if it has substance, then it cannot grant supreme importance to the impartial system, and that system's hold on it will be, at the limit, insecure.

It follows that moral philosophy's habit, particularly in its Kantian forms, of treating persons in abstraction from character is not so much a legitimate device for dealing with one aspect of thought, but is rather a misrepresentation, since it leaves out what both limits and helps to define that aspect of thought. Nor can it be judged solely as a theoretical device: this is one of the areas in which one's conception of the self, and of oneself, most importantly meet.

2 Moral luck

There has been a strain of philosophical thought which identifies the end of life as happiness, happiness as reflective tranquillity, and tranquillity as the product of self-sufficiency – what is not in the domain of the self is not in its control, and so is subject to luck and the contingent enemies of tranquillity. The most extreme versions of this outlook in the Western tradition are certain doctrines of classical antiquity, though it is a notable fact about them that while the good man, the sage, was immune to the impact of incident luck, it was a matter of what may be called constitutive luck that one was a sage, or capable of becoming one: for the many and vulgar this was not (on the prevailing view) an available course.

The idea that one's whole life can in some such way be rendered immune to luck has perhaps rarely prevailed since (it did not prevail, for instance, in mainstream Christianity), but its place has been taken by the still powerfully influential idea that there is one basic form of value, moral value, which is immune to luck and – in the crucial term of the idea's most rigorous exponent – 'unconditioned'. Both the disposition to correct moral judgment, and the objects of such judgment, are on this view free from external contingency, for both are, in their related ways, the product of the unconditioned will. Anything which is the product of happy or unhappy contingency is no proper object of moral assessment, and no proper determinant of it, either.[1] Just as, in the realm of character, it is motive that counts,

---

[1] Kant's own account of this centrally involves the role of the Categorical Imperative. On that issue, I agree with what I take to be the substance of Philippa Foot's position ('Morality as a System of Hypothetical Imperatives', *Phil. Rev.* 1972; and her reply to Frankena, *Philosophy* 1975), but not at all with her way of putting it. In so far as there is a clear distinction between categorical and hypothetical imperatives, and in so far as morality consists of imperatives, it consists of categorical imperatives. The point is that the fact that an imperative is (in this sense) categorical provides no reason at all for obeying it. Nor need Kant think it does: the authority of the

not style, or powers, or endowment, so in action it is not changes actually effected in the world, but intention. With these considerations there is supposed to disappear even that constitutive luck from which the ancient sages were happy to benefit. The capacity for moral agency is supposedly present to any rational agent whatsoever, to anyone for whom the question can even present itself. The successful moral life, removed from considerations of birth, lucky upbringing, or indeed of the incomprehensible Grace of a non-Pelagian God, is presented as a career open not merely to the talents, but to a talent which all rational beings necessarily possess in the same degree. Such a conception has an ultimate form of justice at its heart, and that is its allure. Kantianism is only superficially repulsive – despite appearances, it offers an inducement, solace to a sense of the world's unfairness.

It can offer that solace, however, only if something more is granted. Even if moral value were radically unconditioned by luck, that would not be very significant if moral value were merely one kind of value among others. Rather, moral value has to possess some special, indeed supreme, kind of dignity or importance. The thought that there is a kind of value which is, unlike others, accessible to all rational agents, offers little encouragement if that kind of value is merely a last resort, the doss-house of the spirit. Rather, it must have a claim on one's most fundamental concerns as a rational agent, and in one's recognition of that one is supposed to grasp, not only morality's immunity to luck, but one's own partial immunity to luck through morality.

Any conception of 'moral luck', on this view, is radically incoherent. The phrase indeed sounds strange. This is because the Kantian conception embodies, in a very pure form, something which is basic to our ideas of morality. Yet the aim of making morality immune to luck is bound to be disappointed. The form of this point which is most familiar, from discussions of freewill, is that the dispositions of morality, however far back they are placed in the direction of motive and intention, are as 'conditioned' as anything else. However, the bitter truth (I take it to be both) that morality is subject, after all, to constitutive luck is not what I am going to discuss. The Kantian conception links, and affects, a range of notions: morality, rationality, justification, and ultimate or supreme value. The linkage between those notions, under the Kantian conception, has a number of consequences

Categorical Imperative is supposed (mysteriously enough) to derive not just from its being (in this sense) categorical, but from its being categorical and self-addressed by the agent as a rational being.

for the agent's reflective assessment of his own actions – for instance, that, at the ultimate and most important level, it cannot be a matter of luck whether he was justified in doing what he did.

It is this area that I want to consider. I shall in fact say very little until the end about the moral, concentrating rather on ideas of rational justification. This is the right place to start, I believe, since almost everyone has some commitment to ideas of this kind about rationality and justification, while they may be disposed to think, so far as morality is concerned, that all that is in question is the pure Kantian conception, and that conception merely represents an obsessional exaggeration. But it is not merely that, nor is the Kantian attempt to escape luck an arbitrary enterprise. The attempt is so intimate to our notion of morality, in fact, that its failure may rather make us consider whether we should not give up that notion altogether.

I shall use the notion of 'luck' generously, undefinedly, but, I think, comprehensibly. It will be clear that when I say of something that it is a matter of luck, this is not meant to carry any implication that it is uncaused. My procedure in general will be to invite reflection about how to think and feel about some rather less usual situations, in the light of an appeal to how we – many people – tend to think and feel about other more usual situations, not in terms of substantive moral opinions or 'intuitions' but in terms of the experience of those kinds of situation. There is no suggestion that it is impossible for human beings to lack these feelings and experiences. In the case of the less usual there is only the claim that the thoughts and experiences I consider are possible, coherent, and intelligible, and that there is no ground for condemning them as irrational. In the case of the more usual, there are suggestions, with the outline of a reason for them, that unless we were to be merely confused or unreflective, life without these experiences would involve a much vaster reconstruction of our sentiments and our view of ourselves than may be supposed – supposed, in particular, by those philosophers who discuss these matters as though our experience of our own agency and the sense of our regrets not only could be tidied up to accord with a very simple image of rationality, but already had been.

Let us take first an outline example of the creative artist who turns away from definite and pressing human claims on him in order to live a life in which, as he supposes, he can pursue his art. Without feeling that we are limited by any historical facts, let us call him *Gauguin*. Gauguin might have been a man who was not at all interested in the claims on him, and simply preferred to live another life, and from that life, and perhaps from that preference, his best paintings came. That sort of case, in which the claims of others simply have no hold on the agent, is not what concerns me here, though it serves to remind us of something related to the present concerns, that while we are sometimes guided by the notion that it would be the best of worlds in which morality were universally respected and all men were of a disposition to affirm it, we have in fact deep and persistent reasons to be grateful that that is not the world we have.

Let us take, rather, a Gauguin who is concerned about these claims and what is involved in their being neglected (we may suppose this to be grim), and that he nevertheless, in the face of that, opts for the other life. This other life he might perhaps not see very determinately under the category of realising his gifts as a painter, but, to make things simpler, let us add that he does see it determinately in that light – it is as a life which will enable him really to be a painter that he opts for it. It will then be clearer what will count for him as eventual success in his project – at least, some possible outcomes will be clear examples of success (which does not have to be the same thing as recognition), however many others may be unclear.

Whether he will succeed cannot, in the nature of the case, be foreseen. We are not dealing here with the removal of an external obstacle to something which, once that is removed, will fairly predictably go through. Gauguin, in our story, is putting a great deal on a possibility which has not unequivocally declared itself. I want to explore and uphold the claim that in such a situation the only thing that will justify his choice will be success itself. If he fails – and we shall come shortly to what, more precisely, failure may be – then he did the wrong thing, not just in the sense in which that platitudinously follows, but in the sense that having done the wrong thing in those circumstances he has no basis for the thought that he was justified in acting as he did. If he succeeds, he does have a basis for that thought.

As I have already indicated, I will leave to the end the question of how such notions of justification fit in with distinctively moral ideas. One should be warned already, however, that, even if Gauguin can be ultimately justified, that need not provide him with any way of justifying himself to others, or at least to all others. Thus he may have no way of bringing it about that those who suffer from his decision will have no justified ground of reproach. Even if he succeeds, he will not acquire a right that they accept what he has to say; if he fails, he will not even have anything to say.

The justification, if there is to be one, will be essentially retrospective. Gauguin could not do something which is thought to be essential to rationality and to the notion of justification itself, which is that one should be in a position to apply the justifying considerations at the time of the choice and in advance of knowing whether one was right (in the sense of its coming out right). How this can be in general will form a major part of the discussion. I do not want, at this stage of the argument, to lay much weight on the notion of morality, but it may help to throw some light on the matter of prior justification if we bring in briefly the narrower question whether there could be a prior justification for Gauguin's choice in terms of moral rules.

A moral theorist, recognizing that some value attached to the success of Gauguin's project and hence possibly to his choice, might try to accommodate that choice within a framework of moral rules, by forming a subsidiary rule which could, before the outcome, justify that choice. What could that rule be? It could not be that one is morally justified in deciding to neglect other claims if one is a great creative artist: apart from doubts about its content, the saving clause begs the question which at the relevant time one is in no position to answer. On the other hand, '...if one is convinced that one is a great creative artist' will serve to make obstinacy and fatuous self-delusion conditions of justification, while '...if one is reasonably convinced that one is a great creative artist' is, if anything, worse. What is reasonable conviction supposed to be in such a case? Should Gauguin consult professors of art? The absurdity of such riders surely expresses an absurdity in the whole enterprise of trying to find a place for such cases within the rules.

Utilitarian formulations are not going to contribute any more to understanding these situations than do formulations in terms of rules. They can offer the thought 'it is better (worse) that he did it', where the force of that is, approximately, 'it is better (worse) that it happened', but this in itself does not help towards a characterization of the agent's decision or its possible justification, and Utilitarianism has no special materials of its own to help in that. It has its own well-known problems, too, in spelling out the content of the 'better' – on standard doctrine, Gauguin's decision would seem to have been a better thing, the more popular a painter he eventually became. But there is something more interesting than that kind of difficulty. The Utilitarian perspective, not uniquely but clearly, will miss a very important dimension of such cases, the question of what 'failure' may relevantly be. From the perspective of consequences, the goods or benefits for the sake of which Gauguin's choice was made either materialise in some degree, or do not materialise. But it matters considerably to the thoughts we are considering, in what way the project fails to come off, if it fails. If Gauguin sustains some injury on the way to Tahiti which prevents his ever painting again, that certainly means that his decision (supposing it now to be irreversible) was for nothing, and indeed there is nothing in the outcome to set against the other people's loss. But that train of events does not provoke the thought in question, that after all he was wrong and unjustified. He does not, and never will, know whether he was wrong. What would prove him wrong in his project would not just be that it failed, but that he failed.

This distinction shows that while Gauguin's justification is in some ways a matter of luck, it is not equally a matter of all kinds of luck. It matters how intrinsic the cause of failure is to the project itself. The occurrence of an injury is, relative to these undertakings at least, luck of the most external and incident kind. Irreducibly, luck of this kind affects whether he will be justified or not, since if it strikes, he will not be justified. But it is too external for it to unjustify him, something which only his failure as a painter can do; yet still that is, at another level, luck, the luck of being able to be as he hoped he might be. It might be wondered whether that is *luck* at all, or, if so, whether it may not be luck of that constitutive kind which affects everything and which we have already left on one side. But it is more than that. It is not merely luck that he is such a man, but luck relative to the deliberations that went into his decision, that he turns out to be such a man: he might (epistemically) not have been. That is what sets the problem.

In some cases, though perhaps not in Gauguin's, success in such decisions might be thought not to be a matter of epistemic luck relative to the decision. There might be grounds for saying that the person who was prepared to take the decision, and was in fact right, actually knew that he would succeed, however subjectively uncertain he may have been. But even if this is right for some cases, it does not help with the problems of retrospective justification. For the concept of knowledge here is itself applied retrospectively, and while there is nothing wrong with that, it does not enable the agent at the time of his decision to make any distinctions he could not already make. As one might say, even if it did turn out in such a case that the agent did know, it was still luck, relative to the considerations available to him at the time and at the level at which he made his decision, that he should turn out to have known.

Some luck, in a decision of Gauguin's kind, is extrinsic to his project, some intrinsic; both are necessary for success, and hence for actual justification, but only the latter relates to unjustification. If we now broaden the range of cases slightly, we shall be able to see more clearly the notion of intrinsic luck. In Gauguin's case the nature of the project is such that two distinctions do, roughly, coincide. One is a distinction between luck intrinsic to the project, and luck extrinsic to it; the other is a distinction between what is, and what is not, determined by him and by what he is. The intrinsic luck in Gauguin's case concentrates itself on virtually the one question of whether he is a genuinely gifted painter who can succeed in doing genuinely valuable work. Not all the conditions of the project's coming off lie in him, obviously, since others' actions and refrainings provide many necessary conditions of its coming off – and that is an important locus of extrinsic luck. But the conditions of its coming off which are relevant to unjustification, the locus of intrinsic luck, largely lie in him – which is not to say, of course, that they depend on his will, though some may. This rough coincidence of two distinctions is a feature of this case. But in others, the locus of intrinsic luck (intrinsic, that is to say, to the project) may lie partly outside the agent, and this is an important, and indeed the more typical, case.

Consider an equally schematized account of another example, that of Anna Karenina. Anna remains conscious in her life with Vronsky of the cost exacted from others, above all from her son. She might have lived with that consciousness, we may suppose, if things had gone better, and relative to her state of understanding when she left Karenin, they could have gone better. As it turns out, the social situation and her own state of mind are such that the relationship with Vronsky has to carry too much weight, and the more obvious that becomes, the more it has to carry; and that I take that to be a truth not only about society but about her and Vronsky, a truth which, however inevitable Tolstoy ultimately makes it seem, could, relative to her earlier thoughts, have been otherwise. It is, in the present terms, a matter of intrinsic luck, and a failure in the heart of her project. But its locus is not by any means entirely in her, for it also lies in him.

It would have been an intrinsic failure, also, if Vronsky had actually committed suicide. It would not have been that, but rather an extrinsic misfortune, if Vronsky has been accidentally killed. Though her project would have been at an end, it would not have failed as it does fail. This difference illustrates precisely the thoughts we are concerned with. If Anna had then committed suicide, her thought might have been something like: 'there is nothing more for me'. But I take it that as things are, her thought in killing herself is not just that, but relates inescapably also to the past and to what she has done. What she did, she now finds insupportable, because she could have been justified only by the life she hoped for, and those hopes were not just negated, but refuted, by what happened.

It is such thoughts that I want to place in a structure which will make their sense plainer. The discussion is not in the first place directed to what we or others might say or think of these agents (though it has implications for that), but on what they can be expected coherently to think about themselves. A notion we shall be bound to use in describing their state of mind is *regret*, and there are certain things that need, first, to be said about this notion.

The constitutive thought of regret in general is something like 'how much better if it had been otherwise', and the feeling can in principle apply to anything of which one can form some conception of how it might have been otherwise, together with consciousness of how things would then have been better. In this general sense of regret, what are regretted are states of affairs, and they can be regretted, in principle, by anyone who knows of them. But there is a particularly important species of regret, which I shall call 'agent-regret', which a person can feel only towards his own past actions (or, at most, actions in which he regards himself as a participant). In this case, the supposed possible difference is that one might have acted otherwise, and the focus of the regret is on that possibility, the thought being formed in part by first-personal conceptions of how one might have acted otherwise. 'Agent-regret' is not distinguished from regret in general solely or simply in virtue of its subject-matter. There can be cases of regret directed to one's own past actions which are not cases of agent-regret, because the past action is regarded purely externally, as one might regard anyone else's action. Agent-regret requires not merely a first-personal subject-matter, nor yet merely a particular kind of psychological content, but also a particular kind of expression.

The sentiment of agent-regret is by no means restricted to *voluntary* agency. It can extend far beyond what one intentionally did to almost anything for which one was causally responsible in virtue of something one intentionally did. Yet even at deeply accidental or non-voluntary levels of agency, sentiments of agent-regret are different from regret in general, such as might be felt by a spectator, and are acknowledged in our practice as being different. The lorry driver who, through no fault of his, runs over a child, will feel differently from any spectator, even a spectator next to him in the cab, except perhaps to the extent that the spectator takes on the thought that he himself might have prevented it, an agent's thought. Doubtless, and rightly, people will try, in comforting him, to move the driver from this state of feeling, move him indeed from where he is to something more like the place of a spectator, but it is important that this is seen as something that should need to be done, and indeed some doubt would be felt about a driver who too blandly or readily moved to that position. We feel sorry for the driver, but that sentiment co-exists with, indeed presupposes, that there is something special about his relation to this happening, something which cannot merely be eliminated by the consideration that it was not his fault. It may be still more so in cases where agency is fuller than in such an accident, though still involuntary through ignorance.

The differences between agent-regret and regret felt by a spectator come out not just in thoughts and images that enter into the sentiment, but in differences of expression. The lorry-driver may act in some way which he hopes will constitute or at least symbolise some kind of recompense or restitution, and this will be an expression of his agent-regret. But the willingness to give compensation, even the recognition that one should give it, does not always express agent-regret, and the preparedness to compensate can present itself at very different levels of significance in these connexions. We may recognize the need to pay compensation for damage we involuntarily cause, and yet this recognition be of an external kind, accompanied only by regret of a general kind, or by no regret at all. It may merely be that it would be unfair for the sufferer to bear the cost if there is an alternative, and there is an alternative to be found in the agent whose intentional activities produced the damage as a side-effect.

In these cases, the relevant consciousness of having done the harmful thing is basically that of its having happened as a consequence of one's acts, together with the thought that the cost of its happening can in the circumstances fairly be allocated to one's account. A test of whether that is an agent's state of mind in acknowledging that he should compensate is offered by the question whether from this point of view insurance cover would do at least as well. Imagine the premiums already paid (by someone else, we might add, if that helps to clarify the test): then if knowledge that the victim received insurance payments would settle any unease the agent feels, then it is for him an external case. It is an obvious and welcome consequence of this test that whether an agent can acceptably regard a given case externally is a function not only of his relations to it, but of what sort of case it is – besides the question of whether he should compensate rather than the insurance company, there is the question whether it is the sort of loss that can be compensated at all by insurance. If it is not, an agent conscious that he was unintentionally responsible for it might still feel that he should do something, not necessarily because he could actually compensate where insurance money could not, but because (if he is lucky) his actions might have some reparative significance other than compensation.

In other cases, again, there is no room for any appropriate action at all. Then only the desire to make reparation remains, with the painful consciousness that nothing can be done about it; some other action, perhaps less directed to the victims, may come to express this. What degree of such feeling is appropriate, and what attempts at reparative action or substitutes for it, are questions for particular cases, and that there is room in the area for irrational and self-punitive excess, no one is likely to deny. But equally it would be a kind of insanity never to experience sentiments of this kind towards anyone, and it would be an insane concept of rationality which insisted that a rational person never would. To insist on such a conception of rationality, moreover, would, apart from other kinds of absurdity, suggest a large falsehood: that we might, if we conducted ourselves clear-headedly enough, entirely detach ourselves from the unintentional aspects of our actions, relegating their costs to, so to speak, the insurance fund, and yet still retain our identity and character as agents. One's history as an agent is a web in which anything that is the product of the will is surrounded and held up and partly formed by things that are not, in such a way that reflection can go only in one of two directions: either in the direction of saying that responsible agency is a fairly superficial concept, which has a limited use in harmonizing what happens, or else that it is not a superficial concept, but that it cannot ultimately be purified – if one attaches importance to the sense of what one is in terms of what one has done and what in the world one is responsible for, one must accept much that makes its claim on that sense solely in virtue of its being actual.[2]

The examples of Gauguin and Anna Karenina are, of course, cases of voluntary agency, but they share something with the involuntary cases just mentioned, for the 'luck' of the agents relates to those elements which are essential to the outcome but lie outside their control, and what we are discussing is in this way a very drastic example of determination by the actual, the determination of the agents' judgments on their decisions by what, beyond their will, actually occurs. Besides that, the discussion of agent-regret about the involuntary also helps us to get away from a dichotomy which is often relied on in these matters, expressed in such terms as *regret* and *remorse*, where 'regret' is identified in effect as the regret of the spectator, while 'remorse' is what we have called 'agent-regret', but under the restriction that it applies only to the voluntary. The fact that we have agent-regret about the involuntary, and would not readily recognize a life without it (though we may think we might), shows already that there is something wrong with this dichotomy: such regret is neither mere spectator's regret, nor (by this definition) remorse.

There is a difference between agent-regret as we have so far discussed it, and the agents' feelings in the present cases. As we elicited it from the non-voluntary examples, agent-regret involved a wish on the agent's part that he had not done it. He deeply wishes that he had made that change which, had he known it, was in his power and which would have altered the outcome. But Gauguin or Anna Karenina, as we have represented them, wish they had acted otherwise only if they are unsuccessful. (At least, that wish attends their unsuccess under the simplifying assumption that their subsequent thoughts and feelings are still essentially formed by the projects we have ascribed to them. This is an oversimplication, since evidently they might form new projects in the course of unsuccess itself; though Anna did not. I shall sustain

---

[2] That acceptance is central to tragedy, something which itself presses the question of how we want to think about these things. When Oedipus says 'I did not do it' (Sophocles *Oedipus at Colonus* 539) he speaks as one whose exile and blindness proclaim that he did do it, and to persons who treat him as quite special because he did. Could we have, and do we want, a concept of agency by which what Oedipus said would be simply true, and by which he would be seeing things rightly if for him it was straight off as though he had no part in it? (These questions have little to do with how the law should be: punishment and public amends are a different matter.)

the assumption in what follows.) Whatever feelings these agents had after their decision, but before the declaration of their success or failure, lacked the fully-developed wish to have acted otherwise – that wish comes only when failure is declared.

Regret necessarily involves a wish that things had been otherwise, for instance that one had not had to act as one did. But it does not necessarily involve the wish, all things taken together, that one had acted otherwise. An example of this, largely independent of the present issues, is offered by the cases of conflict between two courses of action each of which is morally required, where either course of action, even if it is judged to be for the best, leaves regrets – which are, in our present terms, agent-regrets about something voluntarily done.³ We should not entirely assimilate agent-regret and the wish, all things taken together, to have acted otherwise. We must now look at some connexions of these to each other, and to certain ideas of justification. This will add the last element to our attempt to characterize our cases.

It will be helpful to contrast our cases with more straightforward cases of practical deliberation and the types of retrospective reflexion appropriate to them. We may take first the simplest cases of pure egoistic deliberation, where not only is the agent's attention confined to egoistic projects, but moral critics would agree that it is legitimately so confined. Here, in one sense the agent does not have to justify his deliberative processes, since there is no one he is answerable to, but it is usually supposed that there is some sense in which even such an agent's deliberative processes can be justified or unjustified – the sense, that is, in which his decision can be reasonable or unreasonable relative to his situation, whatever its actual outcome. Considerations bearing on this include at least the consistency of his thoughts, the rational assessment of probabilities, and the optimal ordering of actions in time.⁴

While the language of justification is used in this connexion, it is less clear than is usually assumed what its content is, and, in particular, what the point is of an agent's being retrospectively concerned with the rationality of his decision, and not just with its success. How are we to understand the retrospective thought of one who comes to see a

³ For some discussion of this see 'Ethical Consistency', in *Problems of the Self* (Cambridge 1973), pp. 166–86.
⁴ A useful outline of such considerations is in D. A. J. Richards, *A Theory of Reasons for Action* (Oxford 1971), ch. 3.

mismatch between his deliberations and the outcome? If he deliberates badly, and as a result of this his projects go wrong, it is easy to see *in that case* how his regret at the outcome appropriately attaches itself to his deliberations. But if he deliberates well, and things go wrong; particularly if, as sometimes happens, they would have gone better if he had deliberated worse; what is the consciousness that he was 'justified' supposed to do for the disposition of his undoubted regret about how things actually turned out? His thought that he was justified seems to carry with it something like this: while he is sorry that things turned out as they did, and, in a sense corresponding to that, he wishes he had acted otherwise, at the same time he does not wish he had acted otherwise, for he stands by the processes of rational deliberation which led to what he did. Similarly with the converse phenomenon, where having made and too late discovered some mistake of deliberation, the agent is by luck successful, and indeed would have been less successful if he had done anything else. Here his gladness that he acted as he did (his lack of a wish to have acted otherwise) operates at a level at which it is compatible with such feelings as self-reproach or retrospective alarm at having acted as he did.

These observations are truisms, but it remains obscure what their real content is. Little is effected by talk of self-reproach or regret at all, still less of co-existent regret and contentment, unless some expression of such sentiments can be identified. Certainly it is not to be identified in this case with any disposition to compensate other persons, for none is affected. Connected with that, criticism by other persons would be on a different basis from criticism offered where they had a grievance, as in a case where an agent risks goods of which he is a trustee, through error, oversight, or (interestingly) merely through the choice of a high-risk strategy to which he would be perfectly entitled if he were acting solely in his own interests. The trustee is not entitled to gamble with the infants' money even if any profits will certainly go to the infants, and success itself will not remove, or start to remove, that objection. That sort of criticism is of course not appropriate in the purely egoistic case, and in fact there is no reason to think that criticism by others is more than a consequential consideration in the egoistic case, derived from others' recommendation of the virtues of rational prudence, which need to be explained first.

Granted that there is no issue of compensation to others in the purely egoistic case, the form of expression of regret seems necessarily to be, as Richards has said,[5] the agent's resolutions for his future deliberations. His regrets about his deliberations express themselves as resolves to think better next time; satisfaction with the deliberation, however disappointing the particular outcome, expresses itself in this, that he finds nothing to be *learned* from the case, and is sure that he will have no better chance of success (at a given level of pay-off) next time by changing his procedures. If this is right, then the notions of regret or lack of regret at the past level of deliberative excellence makes sense only in the context of a policy or disposition of rational deliberation applied to an on-going class of cases.

This is a modest enough conception – it is important to see how modest it is. It implies a class of cases sufficiently similar for deliberative practices to be translated from one to another of them; it does not imply that these cases are all conjointly the subject of deliberative reasoning. I may make a reasoned choice between alternatives of a certain kind today, and, having seen how it turns out, resolve to deal rather differently with the next choice of that kind, but I need not either engage in or resolve to engage in any deliberative reasoning which weighs the options of more than one such occasion together.[6]

Insofar as the outcomes of different such situations affect one another, there is indeed pressure to say that rational deliberation should in principle consider them together. But if one knew enough, virtually any choice would be seen to affect all later ones, so it has seemed to some that the ideal limit of this process is something which is far more ambitious than the modest notion of an ongoing disposition to rational deliberation. This is the model of rational deliberation as directed to a *life-plan*, in Rawls' sense, which treats all times of one's life as of equal concern to one.[7] The theorists of this picture agree that as a matter of fact ignorance and other factors do usually make it rational to discount over remoteness in time, but these are subsequent considerations brought to a model which is that of one's life as a rectangle, so to speak, presented all at once and to be optimally filled in. This

---

[5] Op. cit., pp. 70–1, and cf. ch. 13.

[6] The notion of treating cases together, as opposed to treating them separately but in the light of experience, applies not only to deliberation which yields in advance a conjunctive resolution of a number of cases, but also to deliberation which yields hypothetical conclusions to the effect that a later case will receive a certain treatment if an earlier case turns out in a certain way: as in a staking system.

[7] John Rawls, *A Theory of Justice* (Oxford, 1972), esp. ch. VII; Thomas Nagel, *The Possibility of Altruism* (Oxford, 1970).

model is presented not only as embodying the ideal fulfilment of a rational urge to harmonize all one's projects. It is also supposed to provide a special grounding for the idea that a more fundamental form of regret is directed to deliberative error than to mere mistake. The regret takes the form of self-reproach, and the idea is that we protect ourselves against reproaches from our future self if we act with deliberative rationality: 'nothing can protect us from the ambiguities and limitations of our knowledge, or guarantee that we find the best alternative open to us. Acting with deliberative rationality can only ensure that our conduct is above reproach, and that we are responsible to ourselves as one person over time.'[8] These strains come together in Rawls' advocacy of 'the guiding principle that a rational individual is always to act so that he need never blame himself no matter how things finally transpire'.[9]

Rawls seems to regard this injunction as, in a sense, formal, and as not determining how risky or conservative a strategy the agent should adopt, but it is worth remarking that if any grounding for self-reproach about deliberative error is to be found in the notion of the recriminations of one's later self, the injunction will in fact have to be taken in a more materially cautious sense. The grounding relies on an analogy with the responsibility to other persons: I am a trustee for my own future. If this has any force at all, it is hard to see why it does not extend to my being required, like any other trustee, to adopt a cautious strategy with the entrusted goods – which are, in this case, almost everything I have.

However that may be, the model that gives rise to the injunction is false. Apart from other difficulties,[10] it implicitly ignores the obvious fact that what one does and the sort of life one leads condition one's later desires and judgments. The standpoint of that retrospective judge who will be my later self will be the product of my earlier choices. So there is no set of preferences both fixed and relevant, relative to which the various fillings of my life-space can be compared. If the fillings are to be evaluated by reference to what I variously, in them, want, the relevant preferences are not fixed, while if they are to be evaluated by what I now (for instance) want, this will give a fixed set of preferences, but one that is not necessarily relevant. The recourse from this within the life-space model is to assume (as Utilitarianism

[8] Rawls, pp. 422–3.   [9] p. 422.
[10] It ignores also the very basic fact that the size of the rectangle is up to me: see chapter 1, above.

does) that there is some currency of satisfactions, in terms of which it is possible to compare quite neutrally the value of one set of preferences together with their fulfilments, as against a quite different set of preferences together with their fulfilments. But there is no reason to suppose that there is any such currency, nor that the idea of practical rationality should implicitly presuppose it.

If there is no such currency, then we can only to a limited extent abstract from the projects and preferences we actually have, and cannot in principle gain a standpoint from which the alternative fillings of our life-rectangle could be compared without prejudice. The perspective of deliberative choice on one's life is constitutively *from here*. Correspondingly the perspective of assessment with greater knowledge is necessarily *from there*, and not only can I not guarantee how factually it will then be, but I cannot ultimately guarantee from what standpoint of assessment my major and most fundamental regrets will be.

For many decisions which are part of the agent's ongoing activity (the 'normal science', so to speak, of the moral life) we can see why it is that the presence or absence of regrets is more basically conditioned by the retrospective view of the deliberative processes, than by the particular outcomes. Oneself and one's viewpoint are more basically identified with the dispositions of rational deliberation, applicable to an ongoing series of decisions, than they are with the particular projects which succeed or fail on those occasions. But there are certain other decisions, as in the cases we are considering, which are not like this. There is indeed some room for the presence and subsequent assessment of deliberative rationality. The agents in our cases might well not be taken as seriously as they would otherwise if they did not, to the limited extent that the situation permits, take such rational thought as they can about the realities of their situation. But this is not the aspect under which they will primarily look back on it, nor is it as a contribution to a series of deliberative situations that it will have its importance for them. Though they will learn from it, it will not be in that way. In these cases, the project in the interests of which the decision is made is one with which the agent is identified in such a way that if it succeeds, his stand-point of assessment will be from a life which then derives an important part of its significance for him from that very fact; if he fails, it can, necessarily, have no such significance in his life. If he succeeds, it cannot be that while welcoming the outcome he more basically regrets the decision. If he fails, his standpoint will be of one for whom the ground project of the decision has proved worthless, and this (under the simplifying assumption that other adequate projects are not generated in the process) must leave him with the most basic regrets. So if he fails, his most basic regrets will attach to his decision, and if he succeeds, they cannot. That is the sense in which his decision can be justified, for him, by success.

On this account, it is clear that the decisions we are concerned with are not merely very risky ones, or even very risky ones with a substantial outcome. The outcome has to be substantial in a special way – in a way which importantly conditions the agent's sense of what is significant in his life, and hence his standpoint of retrospective assessment. It follows from this that they are, indeed, risky, and in a way which helps to explain the importance for such projects of the difference between extrinsic and intrinsic failure. With an intrinsic failure, the project which generated the decision is revealed as an empty thing, incapable of grounding the agent's life. With extrinsic failure, it is not so revealed, and while he must acknowledge that it has failed, nevertheless it has not been discredited, and may, perhaps in the form of some new aspiration, contribute to making sense of what is left. In his retrospective thought, and its allocation of basic regret, he cannot in the fullest sense identify with his decision, and so does not find himself justified; but he is not totally alienated from it either, cannot just see it as a disastrous error, and so does not find himself unjustified.

What is the relation of all this, finally, to morality? Does it have any very direct relation? Thomas Nagel,[11] who agrees that morality is deeply and disquietingly subject to luck, denies that an example such as Gauguin's shows that to be so – rather, it shows that Gauguin's most basic retrospective feelings do not have to be moral.

One reason that Nagel gives for this understanding of the matter is that (as I suggested earlier) Gauguin may not be able to justify himself to others, in the sense that they will have no justified grievance. However, this consideration just in itself will not carry great weight unless one makes a strong assumption about the nature of ethical consistency, to the effect that, if someone has acted justifiably from

[11] In his contribution to the symposium for which this paper was originally written: *Proc. Arist. Soc.* Supp. Vol. L (1976), reprinted with revisions in his *Mortal Questions* (Cambridge, 1979). I have benefited from Nagel's paper and from discussion with him. I entirely agree with him that the involvement of morality with luck is not something that can simply be accepted without calling our moral conceptions into question. That was part of my original point; I have tried to state it more directly in the present version of this paper. A difference between Nagel and myself is that I am more sceptical about our moral conceptions than he is.

a moral point of view, then no-one can justifiably complain, from that point of view, of his so acting. But this as a general requirement is unrealistically strong, as can be seen from political cases,[12] for instance, in which we can have reason to approve of the outcome, and of the agent's choice to produce that outcome, and of his being an agent who is able to make that choice, while conscious that there has been a 'moral cost'. It is not reasonable, in such a case, to expect those particular people who have been cheated, used or injured to approve of the agent's action, nor should they be subjected to the patronising thought that, while their complaints are not justified in terms of the whole picture, they are too closely involved to be able to see that truth. Their complaints are, indeed, justified, and they may quite properly refuse to accept the agent's justification which the rest of us may properly accept. The idea that there has been a moral cost itself implies that something bad has been done, and, very often, that someone has been wronged, and if the people who have been wronged do not accept the justification, then no-one can demand that they should. It is for them to decide how far they are prepared to adopt the perspective within which the justification counts. This is just one of the ways – the distancing of time is another – in which, if the moral sentiments are to be part of life as it is actually experienced, they cannot be modelled on a view of the world in which every happening and every person is at the same distance.

Our cases are admittedly different from the case of the politician. There, the justifying conditions relate to issues of what we want effected, what system of government we want, what persons we want to work within that system, and those wants may themselves be shaped by what are, in an everyday sense, moral considerations. With the agents in our examples, it is not the same, and there is, moreover, a difference between the examples themselves. If Gauguin's project succeeds, it can yield a good for the world as Anna's success could not. The moral spectator has to consider the fact that he has reason to be glad that Gauguin succeeded, and hence that he tried – or if a particular spectator finds that he has no disposition to be grateful for Gauguin's paintings, or for paintings, then there will be some other case.

It may be said that this merely represents our gratitude that morality does not always prevail – that moral values have been treated as one value among others, not as unquestionably supreme. I think that that misdescribes our relation to *this* Gauguin, at least, but it is important

[12] See chapter 4, below.

also to bear in mind the grounds, the scope and the significance of that gratitude, which I mentioned earlier, for the limitations of morality. If the moral were really supreme, it would have to be ubiquitous: like Spinoza's substance, if it were to be genuinely unconditioned, there would have to be nothing to condition it.

That is a demand which, only too familiarly, can extend itself among the feelings. The ultimate justice which the Kantian outlook so compellingly demands requires morality, as immune to luck, to be supreme, and while that does not formally require that there be no other sentiments or attachments, in fact it can, like the Robespierrean government to which Heine compared the Kantian system in general, steadily grow to require a wider conformity of the sentiments. Justice requires not merely that *something I am* should be beyond luck, but that *what I most fundamentally am* should be so, and, in the light of that, admiration or liking or even enjoyment of the happy manifestations of luck can seem to be treachery to moral worth. That guilty levelling of the sentiments can occur even if one recognizes, as Kant recognized, that there are some things that one is responsible for, and others for which one is not. The final destruction occurs when the Kantian sense of justice is joined to a Utilitarian conception of negative responsibility, and one is left, at any level of importance, only with purely moral motivations and no limit to their application. There is, at the end of that, no life of one's own, except perhaps for some small area, hygienically allotted, of meaningless privacy.

Because that is a genuine pathology of the moral life, the limitation of the moral is itself something morally important. But to regard Gauguin's decision simply as a welcome incursion of the amoral is anyway too limited. It will be adequate only if he is the amoral Gauguin we put aside at the beginning. If he is not, then he is himself open to regrets for what he has done to others, and, if he fails, then those regrets are not only all that he has, but, as I have tried to explain, he no longer even has the perspective within which something else could have been laid against them. That can make a difference to the moral spectator. While he may admire the amoral Gauguin's achievements, and indeed admire him, this other Gauguin is someone who shares the same world of moral concerns. The risk these agents run is a risk within morality, a risk which amoral versions of these agents would not run at all.

The fact that these agents' justifications, if they acquired them, would not properly silence all complaints, does not itself lead to the conclusion that they are not moral justifications. However, perhaps we should, all the same, accept that conclusion. Their moral luck, we should then say, does not lie in acquiring a moral justification. It lies rather in the relation of their life, and of their justification or lack of it, to morality. That relation has to be seen in the first instance in their perspective, one in which, if they fail, there is simply regret. But their life is recognizably part of moral life, and it has a significance for us as well.

There is now, however, a pressing question – how much is being done by the concept of the moral, and how much *by this stage of the argument* does it matter what happens to it? In reminding ourselves of the significance of luck to the moral life – whether it is constitutive luck, or that which affects the relations of one's decisions to morality, or that which affects merely what one will turn out to have done – we essentially use the concept, because we are working out in reflection from central applications of the concept to question what may be a basic motive for using it at all:[13] the motive of establishing a dimension of decision and assessment which can hope to transcend luck. Once that motive is understood and questioned, it has to be asked once more what the concept is for, and, by the same token, how many other features of it can be taken for granted.

Scepticism about the freedom of morality from luck cannot leave the concept of morality where it was, any more than it can remain undisturbed by scepticism about the very closely related image we have of there being a moral order, within which our actions have a significance which may not be accorded to them by mere social recognition. These forms of scepticism will leave us with *a* concept of morality, but one less important, certainly, than ours is usually taken to be; and that will not be ours, since one thing that is particularly important about ours is how important it is taken to be.

[13] As Nagel points out, the situation resembles to some degree that with scepticism about knowledge. The same idea indeed seems to be involved in both cases: the knower is one whose belief is non-accidentally true (for discussion, see my *Descartes: the Project of Pure Enquiry* (Harmondsworth, 1978), pp. 37 seq). However, the path taken by scepticism from these similar starting points, and its eventual effectiveness, seem to me very different in the two cases.

3   Utilitarianism and moral self-indulgence

My problem arises from the question of what one is to do in circumstances where there are strong reasons, particularly of a utilitarian kind, for doing something which one finds morally distasteful, and against which one has a strong personal commitment. It also of course involves questions of what one says and thinks about other people's actions in such situations. My concern is with a charge that can be brought against people who reject morally distasteful acts in such cases, namely that they are guilty of a certain kind of self-indulgence. When the agent's refusal takes the particular form of saying that while others, no doubt, will bring evil about, at least it will not come about through *him*, the charge may handily take the form of saying that the agent displays a possessive attitude towards his own virtue.[1]

The problem particularly comes up in relation to utilitarianism. If the reasons for the act are, from a utilitarian point of view, strong enough, then utilitarians will say that the fact that the act is morally distasteful is certainly not an adequate reason against doing it in this case; as a general characteristic of acts of this sort, it is largely irrelevant to questions of what to do here and now, though it may be relevant to other aspects of the situation – thus we may think well of the agent for finding this kind of act distasteful, his reaction being taken as a reassuring sign of good character. It is in the context of a critique of utilitarianism that I have elsewhere[2] invoked the notion of *integrity* in this connexion, and it is in this context that I shall discuss the problem here, taking, that is to say, the reasons inviting one to the distasteful act as utilitarian reasons. However, the general structure of this problem for individual action is not confined to this sort of case, and I hope that my discussion will help to bring that out.

---

[1] The phrase appears in a discussion of these issues by Jonathan Glover, *Proc. Arist. Soc.*, Supplementary Volume XLIX (1975).

[2] In J. J. C. Smart and B. Williams, *Utilitarianism: For and Against* (CUP, 1973).

There is a set of problems very closely related to this one, which are problems of politics – taking this in a broad sense of action in a public capacity in a public domain, though the clearest and most important issues arise from matters of state. The clearest of all cases are actions by politicians in the exercise of their office in the context of international affairs, but similar issues can range down to such matters as rising politicians making deals to advance their careers, and their aspirations, and their supporters' moral hopes. These problems of political morality – the matter of 'dirty hands'[3] – I shall not try to discuss here. It is important that they are not just a special case of the issue I shall discuss, not just examples of that issue arising in the political domain. In the clearest examples of the political, we have two special features. First, the agent stands in a relation to others – citizens, supporters, electors, etc. – in which he is supposed to effect results which involve, and can be known to involve, such acts; and this relation itself can have a moral dimension, for instance of trust. I say 'is supposed to effect results which involve...' rather than 'is supposed to perform such acts' because the public sometimes do take, and the media often pretend to take, a moralised view by which politicians are supposed not to do the acts required for what they are supposed to achieve. Second, the sphere of operation is itself less moralised and less structured by moralised expectations than at least a lot of other activities in at least settled communities: international relations are of course the prime example of this.

These two factors are different from one another. Issues of the second kind might arise even if there were no-one you were responsible to and for: some, though not all, traditional moralists have thought that there were restrictions on the extent to which moral considerations apply in the state of nature, and believed in the moral analogue to *silent leges inter arma*. The first feature, again, can arise without the second, but without the second factor, there would be greater doubt that the role being exercised by those responsible was a legitimate or acceptable role – the expectations people have of the leader are affected by their perception of the terrain over which he is leading them.

For these reasons, questions of dirty hands are not just a special case of the present problem: or rather, to assume that they are is to beg a major question about the answer to them. The present problem is about the nature and proper content of what is undoubtedly a person's

---

[3] See Michael Walzer's discussion in *Philosophy and Public Affairs* (Winter, 1973); and chapter 4, below.

individual moral judgement, and (leaving aside an outlook which actually *defined* moral considerations in terms of utilitarianism) concerns what is certainly a moral choice between moral solutions. The question of dirty hands, at least in its strongest form, concerns what role a person's individual moral judgement is supposed to play in the business at all. The present problem is interested in the individual's moral consciousness and how it should appreciate the situation; the question of dirty hands raises the issue of whether his moral consciousness, and how it appreciates the situation, is not just an irrelevance.

One issue that does notably arise with both these questions, but which, again, I shall not discuss, is the extent to which, and the ways in which, actions offensive to morality can be retrospectively justified – perhaps even morally justified – by success; and what, if they can, may count as success. In its least palatable form, this is the view that even political atrocities can be justified by history. However, neither the unpalatableness of that application, nor (still less) some supposed guarantee offered by the sense of the term 'moral', should lead us to underestimate this view in general: it has more to it than people like to admit. But it is a topic for another occasion.

Our problem arises with cases in which the agent is faced with a reliable choice between a detestable action and an outcome which will be utilitarianly worse: where 'a reliable choice' means that he has a choice between doing and not doing the action, and it is certain beyond reasonable doubt that if he does not do the action, then that outcome, or something yet worse than that outcome, will follow.[4] There are familiar arguments to suggest that no, or few, such choices are in fact reliable. On the one hand, utilitarians urge the importance of side-effects in calculating the balance of utility between acting and refraining: when side-effects are included, the detestable action will be said to possess less utility than at first appearance, and may have less utility than the alternative outcome. It is worth remarking that the level of probability attaching to these considerations is usually left quite indeterminate. Some of these effects, on which great weight in the abstract is put by defenders of utilitarianism, are so problematical that in any actual case a consistent and clear-headed utilitarian would be bound very largely to discount them. In any case, we shall assume that

---

[4] It can be accepted, presumably, that the more horrible the action which is to be justified by the prospect of a given good outcome, the more probable it has to be that the outcome will indeed follow the action: suppose this already allowed for in the case. For two examples of the kind in question, see Smart and Williams, op. cit., pp. 97–9.

we are dealing with a class of cases in which, when all these considerations are counted in, the balance of utilitarian advantage favours the (otherwise) detestable action. Clearly no utilitarian could say, and few would want to, that there could not be any such case.

An alternative tack for casting doubt on the reliability of such choices, used this time by anti-utilitarians, is to suggest that the efficacy of the detestable action (e.g in preventing great harms which would otherwise occur) is more doubtful than the example supposes. This is a line often taken by those defending an absolutist position in cases of detestable actions extorted by threats made by hijackers and so forth, to the effect that the very character of the threat shows that one has reason to doubt the efficacy of giving in to it: why should one expect such threateners to keep their promises anyway? As a *general* line of argument, this seems to me, bluntly, a cop-out. Of course there are some cases in which it is a reasonable bet that nothing is to be gained by giving in to threats, but there are others in which it is not a reasonable bet, and it is merely an evasion to pretend that we have an *a priori* assurance, applicable to every case, that it is inadequately certain that the action will have its expected effect.[5]

In any case, there are only certain sorts of examples to which this line of reasoning can be relevantly applied at all, namely those in which, if the threateners fail to deliver, the all-round outcome is worse than if one had not done the detestable action. Not all cases which raise our problem − not even all that involve threateners − are of this structure. There is the case in which I am invited to kill one man, and told that if I refuse, someone else will shoot that man and several other men as well. If we think solely in terms of outcomes, then the only conceivable outcome actually better than those which involve my accepting, is that in which I refuse and they decide not to kill anyone; but there is absolutely no probability of that at all. If the other persons do what is analogous to promise-breaking in a hijacking case, namely that I accept and they nevertheless kill the rest, then the outcome, regarded as an outcome, is only the same as what it certainly will be if I refuse. So in terms of outcomes, we need only some non-zero

---

[5] The underlying idea seems to be the *unity of the vices*, a psychologically unsound principle. A bizarre application of much the same idea is an argument adopted by P. T. Geach from McTaggart, to the effect that we could have no reason to believe in an unjust hell: the only ground for belief in hell being revelation, we should have no reason to regard as trustworthy the communications of a God wicked enough to run an unjust hell. See *Providence and Evil* (Cambridge 1977), pp. 134–6.

probability that they will do what they say for my acceptance to be rational.

In general, arguments of this kind seem only too ready to confuse the idea that some factor ignored in the example is possible, with the idea that it has some indeterminately high probability. In this, they notably resemble some arguments brought forward by their utilitarian opponents. No doubt the reason is the same: each in its own way is trying to find a consequentialist argument for some sentiment which does not have its roots in consequentialist considerations at all.

Let us then grant a reliable choice of the kind in question. Someone who knowingly takes the anti-utilitarian course in such a case might be open to the charge of being concerned with his own integrity or purity or virtue at others' expense. To use one phrase as a general label, though it might not always be the best phrase, let us call this the charge of moral self-indulgence. The first things I want to discuss are certain necessary conditions of such a charge being appropriate. In doing this, I shall assume that this charge is not, and is not intended to be, just trivially *equivalent* to a disapproving claim that someone, for reasons of the moral kind, knowingly acted in an anti-utilitarian way. I take it that an equivalence is not intended, since one who makes this charge in this connexion surely intends to commend the utilitarian solution to such cases, and hence indirectly the utilitarian system, by bringing non-utilitarian outlooks in certain of their applications under a charge which has some independent force, and which might already be recognised as an objection. It is this independent force which I shall try to uncover; and I shall, more particularly, assume that the charge of moral self-indulgence imputes a specific kind of *motive*.

It is, in fact, neither a sufficient nor a necessary condition of this charge's being appropriate that the agent knowingly does from a motive of the moral kind something which is counter-utilitarian. It is not sufficient, for consider the case of a man who, courageously doing what he takes to be his duty (or even just courageously), gets himself killed in the course of a counter-utilitarian project. He may be rash or foolish, but not, on the strength of this, morally self-indulgent: what contributes to this may possibly include the fact that he pays a high price himself. It is also not a necessary condition. It is possible for someone to be open to the charge of moral self-indulgence when the moral considerations which influence him are themselves utilitarian ones. Someone might incur this charge in certain cases (not all) who, for reasons of the general utilitarian welfare, left high and dry someone who depended on him. If the man who refused to shoot when invited to by the threateners was keeping his hands clean from what the utilitarian would regard as ultimately unreal dirt, *this* man is keeping his hands clean from what, for the utilitarian, is real dirt.

What would encourage one to bring this charge against this man? One feature might be that he did not really seem to care about any particular other beneficiaries very much. This cannot mean just that there were no particularly identified beneficiaries about whom he cared – *that* would be the case with, for instance, a man who honourably acted in the interests of the unidentified inhabitants of an identified town, or, to take a more radical case, acted to prevent radiation hazard to future people. Nor will refinements on this thought get us to the nub of the charge; but the thought is suggestive of something which is much nearer the nub of the charge. One thing the thought can express is the suspicion that what the agent cares about is not so much other people, as himself caring about other people. He has an image of himself as a virtuous utilitarian, and this image is more important in his motivation than any concern for other persons, in particular that person for whom he is specially invited to show concern.

It is this type of *reflexive* concern which, I suggest, is significantly related to the charge of moral self-indulgence. It can arise with any moral motivation whatsoever. Thus a person may act from generosity or loyalty, and act in a counter-utilitarian way, and not attract the charge of moral self-indulgence, but that charge will be attracted if the suspicion is that his act is motivated by a concern for his own generosity or loyalty, the enhancement or preservation of his own self-image as a generous or loyal person. In the case of a man who acts in a counter-utilitarian way for reasons not of the moral kind, the charge of moral self-indulgence will not in any case stick, since ‘moral’ is not the sort of self-indulgence, if any, that he is going in for. But there are highly analogous contrasts in the matter of reflexivity. It is one thing for a man to act in a counter-utilitarian way out of his great love for Isolde, another for him to do so out of a concern for his image of himself as a great Tristan. The distinction applies even to the case of selfishness. One can act selfishly, that is to say, in a manner motivated by desire of things for oneself and indifferently to the welfare of others, but it would be different from that to act from a conception of oneself as a person who so acts. While the latter is unlikely to be nicer, it has a chance of being a bit grander.

I take it that there is in general a clear conceptual distinction between the first-order motivation in each of these cases, and its reflexive second-order substitute. After that very general recognition, however, there are many respects in which even at the analytical level, let alone in psychological reality, boundaries are quite unclear. I shall make one or two remarks on what is obviously a large set of questions.

One necessary condition of ascribing the second-order motivation to an agent is that we also take him to possess the concept of the first-order motivation in question. A particularly clear distinction between the two types of motivation is available where it is possible to be motivated in a certain moral way without possessing the relevant concept of that motivation at all. Some types of virtuous motivation permit this, and it is one more mistaken consequence of Kantian moral theory that the only genuine moral motivation is taken to to be one which essentially involves the agent's being conscious of that type of motivation. But even if an agent does possess the concept of a certain virtuous motivation, it may be that he does not apply it to his own case: in the space provided, with some virtues, by this possibility, there is room for such a thing as intelligent innocence. And even if, last, the concept is applied and the thought of his own disposition is present, that is not the same as his motivation being provided by that thought. It is a point worth further inquiry that in the case of some virtues (such as, perhaps, courage) the presence of such a thought may be encouraging to the first-order motivation, whereas with others it is not so, the presence of the thought tending to destroy the first-order motivation. To the extent that this latter is so, there will be a reason (there are others) why some virtues are only imperfectly accessible to highly self-conscious and reflective agents, as there are other virtues fully accessible only to them.

It may well be that the route to acquiring and sustaining the first-order virtuous motivations requires a kind of self-esteem which may involve to some degree and in some form second-order motivations. It is a question of psychological theory to what extent that is so, though that extent is certainly limited, for instance by the matters of concept-possession which have already been mentioned. It is a psychological matter also, less perhaps of theory than of common observation, to what extent what sort of motive actually operates. Nothing I say is meant to imply that it is in the least easy to tell to what degree what sort of motive is operating, in someone else's case or – what in the nature of this matter is a very different thing – one's own.

However, even if there is a difference between these sorts of motivations, there remains a question about what, if anything, is supposed to be wrong with the second-order motivation – in particular, what about it makes it self-indulgent. Indeed, some philosopher might argue that for at least some kinds of second-order motivation there could not be anything wrong with it. For on the account given so far, it looks as though a man would be motivated in some such second-order way if he were to ask himself 'What would I do if I acted as a generous man would act here?', and were motivated to act on the answer; and if he gave the right answer to the question, and acted on it, then it looks as though he would do just what a generous man would do, and for no worse reason. Is that moral self-indulgence?

No; though as a picture of moral deliberation the pattern is surely very distorted (whether the distortion is in the picture or in what is pictured). What is lacking from this for it to be, however odd in other ways, a matter of self-indulgence is some element of self-esteem – a point suggested by the fact that it is, after all, the generosity of some hypothetical ideally generous person that is invoked here, not the agent's own. Here we can be misled by phrases such as 'he is concerned with being generous'. This may mean merely that he is concerned to do the generous thing in a sense in which that is what any generous man is concerned to do; or that he is concerned to conform his conduct to some paradigm of a generous man, like the agent just mentioned (this kind of reflexivity looks, in fact, like a familiar example of a more primitive, rather than a fuller, moral development); or it may mean that he is concerned with his own generosity, where this implies that he had substituted for a thought about what is needed, a thought which focuses disproportionately upon the expression of his own disposition, and that he derives pleasure from the thought that his disposition will have been expressed – rather than deriving pleasure, as the agent who is not self-indulgent may, from the thought of how things will be if he acts in a certain way, that way being (though he need not think this) the expression of his disposition.

It is this sort of reflexivity which invites the name 'self-indulgence'. It involves a reversal at a line which I take to be fundamental to any morality or indeed sane life at all, between self-concern and other-concern; it involves a misdirection not just of attention, though that is true too, but genuinely of concern, and they both issue in differences in what actually gets done. Distortions which are due primarily to diverted attention, are familiar also with skills; those which come from diverted concern, the virtues share with the affections. These differences in what gets done fit in with something noted earlier in the matter of courage, the evidential weight attached in these questions to the agent's himself paying a price; he *can* do that in the course of reflexively regarding his own virtue, but the space for it becomes more constricted.

These remarks about reflexivity and moral motivation involve a claim about a question which is hard and important and has been inadequately studied: how we are to picture the expression of moral dispositions in an agent's deliberative thought. We have some views in philosophy about the reference to dispositions in explaining and evaluating other people's conduct. We have some views about the occurrence of moral considerations in practical deliberation (though they are largely restricted to questions about the function in deliberation of 'moral judgements'). What we seem to lack is any coherent representation of something which is certainly true, that distinctive moral dispositions, such as generosity, are expressed in the content (and not just the occasions) of the agent's deliberations. The one claim that I make about that subject here is that the characteristic and basic expression of a moral disposition in deliberation is *not* a premiss which refers to that disposition – it is not the basic characteristic of a generous man's deliberations that they use the premiss 'I am a generous man'. Whatever one goes on to say about this subject, that negative claim is surely correct. Though the generous man is partly characterised by what goes into his deliberations, it is not that what goes into them are reflections on his generosity.[6]

We are now in a position to see better the relations between utilitarianism and integrity in the matter of moral self-indulgence. If the objectionable feature of moral self-indulgence is identified as a certain kind of reflexive motivation, then it cannot stand in any simple contrast with utilitarian motivation. For, first, it can be contrasted with many things other than utilitarian motivation – as, in general, with first-order virtuous motivations. Further, utilitarian benevolence is

[6] Nor, we can add, is it merely thoughts such as 'he needs help'; the occurrence of such thoughts certainly mark out some men from others, but does little to mark out generous men from non-generous. Nor is it the 'moral judgement', 'I ought to help'; apart from well-known questions about the connexion of that with motivation, it is not specially the mark of a generous man to have or act on that thought. An answer will probably have to start from the idea that the basic representation in deliberation of such a disposition is in the form 'I want to help...'; this has the further advantage of not making it unintelligible how such moral considerations can be weighed in deliberation against quite different considerations.

itself open to this reflexive deformation. The reason why utilitarian motivation seems to many the unique enemy of moral self-indulgence is that it seems the purest expression of other-concern as opposed to self-concern – isn't utilitarianism just the expression of concern for everyone, among whom self is outnumbered by others? But in fact the distinction between other-concern and self-concern is in no way the same thing as the distinction between utilitarian and non-utilitarian, and in the sense in which other-concerned motivations which are not those of utilitarianism are capable of reflexive deformation into one kind of self-concern, so is utilitarian motivation itself.

What about concern with one's own *integrity*? The simplest thing to say about this would be that integrity is one case of a virtue, and that, like other virtues, it is subject to reflexive deformation. But I think that this would be wrong; rather, one should perhaps say that integrity is not a *virtue* at all. In saying that, I do not mean that there is not all that much to be said for it, as one might say that humility was not a virtue. I mean that while it is an admirable human property, it is not related to motivation as the virtues are. It is not a disposition which itself yields motivations, as generosity and benevolence do; nor is it a virtue of that type, sometimes called 'executive' virtues, which do not themselves yield a characteristic motive, but are necessary for that relation to oneself and the world which enables one to act from desirable motives in desirable ways – the type that includes courage and self-control. It is rather that one who displays integrity acts from those dispositions and motives which are most deeply his, and has also the virtues that enable him to do that. Integrity does not enable him to do it, nor is it what he acts from when he does so.

If that is right, we can see why integrity, regarded as a virtue, can seem to smack of moral self-indulgence. For if it is regarded as a motive, it is hard to reconstruct its representation in thought except in the objectionable reflexive way: the thought would have to be about oneself and one's own character, and of the suspect kind. If integrity had to be provided with a characteristic thought, there would be nothing for the thought to be about except oneself – but there is no such characteristic thought, only the thoughts associated with the projects, in carrying out which a man may display his integrity. Relatedly, one cannot directly bring someone up to possess integrity, in the sense of teaching him to display or exercise it; rather one brings it about that he genuinely cares for something and has the characteristics necessary to live in the spirit of that.

But what of the thought 'not through me' – the thought that even if others are going to bring evil and injustice into the world, it will not be by my agency that it comes about?[7] This, certainly, is already a reflexive thought, and involves at least one step away from the simply unselfconscious expression of counter-utilitarian dispositions. The thought, however, is not in itself a motivating thought, and those words do not express any distinctive motivation. It is not merely that they do not on all occasions express some one motivation. Rather, they do not, in themselves, express any motivation at all: if one is motivated *not to do it oneself*, then there is some (other) motive one has for not doing it. One such motive is fear, and in the particular form, perhaps, of the fear of pollution, it can attract the accusation of cowardice to some agents in the sort of circumstances we are discussing. With the motivation of fear in general, it is often the case that the agent *would prefer to be able to do* whatever it is he fears doing. In relation to that, the fear of pollution is a special case, providing either an exception to it, or a peculiarly complex instance of it. But in any case, fear, of whatever kind, is by no means always the motive of agents who use those words.

A quite different, perhaps limiting, case of a motive lying behind those words would be one related to pride, the motive of one of whom it is not true that he would prefer to be able to do it – he could do it – but who does not want it done, and refuses to be made to do it by another's providing him with reasons for doing it. A bare, unsupported motive of this kind could hardly be adequate to the cases we have in mind – because the interests of innocent parties have been thrown into the reasons for acting, this would be, too much, arbitrary self-assertion. But a similar, though different, thought can be expressed by the agent in our case: similar, in that he registers a refusal to be coerced by the threats, inducements or example of others; different in that he is not just asserting his own independence and right to refuse, but expressing the other motivations he has for not doing the act in question.

Utilitarians will, or course, dispute his right to refuse, but the point is that the agent's affirmation 'not through me' does not, in such a case, express a motivation of the suspect, 'self-indulgent', kind. In itself, it does not represent any motivation at all, and the motivations which

---

[7] Glover, op. cit., has called this the 'Solzhenitsyn principle', after a passage in that writer's Nobel oration. The name is well invoked; but this thought should not be regarded as a *principle*.

can lie behind it include some which are, for various reasons, suspect and some which are not. The reflexivity of the utterance does not represent in itself any suspect motive, but only the self-consciousness of the refusal, however the refusal is motivated.

There are many and various forms of dispositions, patterns of feeling and desire, which can motivate people to counter-utilitarian acts; some themselves virtues, some more particular projects, affections and commitments. The question I turn to last is the place that utilitarianism can allow to such dispositions. They can be variously admired or deplored, cultivated or discouraged. Some may indeed be admired and encouraged for what are, remotely and ultimately, utilitarian reasons, in the sense that human welfare is served indirectly by the presence of these dispositions in the world. I think that it is wrong to try to reduce all questions of the assessment of such dispositions to utilitarian considerations, and indeed that it is incoherent, since there is no coherent view of human welfare itself which is independent of such issues as what people care for, in non-utilitarian spirit, with regard to such things as these dispositions. But that is not my concern here, and if the present argument goes through for those dispositions of this type which can be granted indirect utilitarian value, then it will presumably have some *ad hominem* force against utilitarianism.

The difficulty is that such dispositions are patterns of motivation, feeling and action, and one cannot have both the world containing these dispositions, and its actions regularly fulfilling the requirements of utilitarianism. If you are a person who whole-heartedly and genuinely possesses some of these admirable dispositions, you cannot also be someone in whose thought and action the requirements of utilitarianism are unfailingly mirrored, nor could you wish to be such a person. If you want the world to contain generous, affectionate, forceful, resolute, creative and actually happy people, you do not wish it to contain people who uniformly think in such a way that their actions will satisfy the requirements of utilitarianism.

The supposition that one might combine the dispositions one wants and admires in the world with actions that maximally satisfy the utilitarian criterion stems from a number of errors. One is an idea, which utilitarianism, though it denies it, is in fact disposed to share with other pictures of moral experience, and indeed of practical rationality in general, that the processes of practical thought are transcendental to experience and do not actually take up any psychological room. But in fact to think in one way rather than another about what to do is to be empirically different, to be a certain kind of person, and it is not possible to combine all kinds of reflection with all kinds of disposition. Utilitarians neglect this to some extent at the level of the individual, but they have made a speciality out of neglecting it at the social level, supposing for instance that there could be an élite of utilitarian thinkers who possessed an esoteric doctrine unknown to others, without there being specified any form of social organisation to make this structure a social reality.

Second, there is the error, also shared with others, of dissociating moral thought and decision from moral feeling. It is a commonplace that there is a form of weakness which consists in being overcome by unstructured moral feeling and there is another which consists in a kind of squeamishness. These are often failures of confusion, of lack of self-knowledge. But the cure for them cannot or should not consist in teaching people to discount their moral feelings, to dissociate themselves from them.[8] Theorists who encourage this are fond of such cases as that of the lapsed and now unbelieving Catholic who feels guilty when he does not go to Mass. But whatever is to be said about that case, it cannot be a paradigm of what the utilitarian needs. The lapsed Catholic aims to dissociate himself entirely from the Mass and its claims, to reach a position from which no such feeling has any significance at all. But no such thing is true of the man involved in counter-utilitarian feelings in a case such as we are discussing. These feelings represent something he in general stands by, and which the utilitarian, we are supposing, wants him in general to stand by.

No one is suggesting that moral feeling should express itself unmodified by thought (at the limit, this is not even a comprehensible idea). There are, further, some moral feelings, particularly concerned with the observance of rules, which can be formed by experience in ways which to some extent fit round and accommodate utilitarian thoughts: it is so, up to a point, with the rules of promise-keeping and truth-telling. But there is no reason at all to believe, for many dispositions of the kind that it is desirable to have in the world, that

[8] A theory of the moral sentiments in needed here. One approach to the questions of dissociation from moral feeling might be suggested by a certain contrast between moral feeling and sense-perception. Those views, of rationalist type, which most strongly advocate dissociation from perceptual sensations, at least emphasise a truth, that the aim of objective knowledge is to dissociate thought about the world, certainly from what is distinctively oneself, and perhaps (on realist views) from anything that is distinctively human. But that cannot be the aim of moral thought and experience, which must primarily involve grasping the world in such a way that one can, as a particular human being, live in it.

they can retain their position and significance and yet systematically make way, whenever required to, for the deliverances of utilitarian thought, the feelings associated with the disposition being made the objects of dissociation.

Relatedly, there is not much to be got out of a third line of thought, which can also encourage an oversimple view of these problems, the supposedly clear distinction between judging the act and judging the agent. If a man has a disposition of a kind which it is good that he has, and if what he did was just what a man with such a disposition would be bound to do in such a case, but (as I claim must sometimes be so) was counter-utilitarian: what is the force of saying that what he did was as a matter of fact wrong? It is important that it does *not* have the force – which really would give some point to the distinction of act and agent – that, if he had been in a position to conduct his deliberations better, he would have acted differently. He conducted his deliberations as such a man does, and it is good that he is such a man. By the same token, it cannot mean that we ought to try to bring people up to be such that they do not make such mistakes. If there is any content to saying that this man did the wrong thing, it must be compatible with our thinking that it is a good thing that people do not always do the right thing; and not just in the very general sense in which we may reflect on the uncovenanted benefits which can flow even from dire acts, but in the more intimate sense that we want the world to contain people who when they ask themselves 'what is the right thing to do?' will, on definitely specifiable sorts of occasion, give the wrong answer.

The utilitarian's theory, once he admits the value of these dispositions, takes the question 'what is the right thing to do?' a long way away from the question 'what answers is it desirable that people should be disposed to give to the question "what is the right thing to do?"?' The tension created by this separation is very great, and there is very strong pressure, if utilitarianism is to retain any distinct identity *within* moral thought, for it to reject or hopelessly dilute the value of these other dispositions, regressing to that picture of man which early utilitarianism frankly offered, in which he has, ideally, only private or otherwise sacrificeable projects, together with the one moral disposition of utilitarian benevolence. I hope to have shown that that false picture cannot be commended to us by rejecting other moral motivations, in their counter-utilitarian appearances, as pieces of moral self-indulgence.

4   Politics and moral character

What sorts of person do we want and need to be politicians? This question, and the broader question of what we morally want from politics, are importantly different from the question of what the correct answers are to moral problems which present themselves within political activity. We may want – we may *morally* want – politicians who on some occasions ignore those problems. Moreover, even in cases where what we want the politician to do is to consider, and give the right answer to, such a problem, it is not enough to say that we want him to be the sort of person who can do that. Since some of the correct answers involve actions which are nonetheless very disagreeable, further questions arise about the sorts of persons who will give – in particular, who may find it too easy to give – those right answers.

I am concerned with cases where the politician does something morally disagreeable, and with the problem that has been called that of *dirty hands*. The central question is: how are we to think about the involvement of politicians in such actions, and about the dispositions that such involvement requires? This is not in the first place a question about what is permissible and defensible in such connexions, though something, obviously, will have to be said about what it means to claim that a politician has adequate reason to do something which is, as I put it, 'morally disagreeable'.

The discussion assumes that it makes some difference what politicians are like, what dispositions they have. I do not want to stress an individualist picture of political action too much, but I assume that there is something to be said in the moral dimension about the actions of individual politicians. Even someone who denied this might admit, I suppose, that it could make some difference, of the sort that concerns us morally, what politicians were like. Someone who denies all that will probably think that morality has nothing to do with politics at all, and for him the whole area of discussion lapses.

It is widely believed that the practice of politics selects at least for cynicism and perhaps for brutality in its practitioners. This belief, and our whole subject, notoriously elicit an uncertain tone from academics, who tend to be either over-embarrassed or under-embarrassed by moralising in the face of power. Excited, in either direction, by the subject, they often take rather large-scale or epic examples, such as the conduct of international relations by hostile powers, or ruthless policies which may or may not be justified by history. I will touch marginally on those kinds of issue at the end, but my first concern is more with the simply squalid end of the subject, and with the politician not so much as national leader or maker of history, but as professional. I shall defer the more heady question of politicians being criminals in favour of the more banal notion that they are crooks.

There is of course one totally banal sense of the claim that they are crooks, namely that some break the law for their own advantage, take bribes, do shady things which are not actually illegal for personal gain. This dimension of effort is for the present purpose mostly beside the point. It does raise one or two interesting questions, for instance the absence from politics of any very robust notion of professional ethics. Some professions, such as lawyers and doctors, have elaborate codes of professional ethics. I take it that this is not because their vocation rises nobly above any thoughts of personal gain, but because their clients need to be protected, and be seen to be protected, in what are particularly sensitive areas of their interests. Some areas of business have similar provisions, but in general the concept of a professional business ethic is less developed than that of a professional medical or legal ethic. One might think that politics was concerned quite generally with sensitive areas of the clients' interests, yet even in places where it is recognized that these restrictions govern the activities of doctors and lawyers, the politician's professional conduct is perceived as more like that of the business man. The explanation of this fact I take not to be very mysterious: roughly, there are several reasons why it is in the interest of most in these professions to belong to a respectable cartel, but in the case of politicians, the circumstances in which they are able to run a cartel are circumstances in which they have little motive to keep it respectable.

How are the morally dubious activities which belong to this, irrelevant, class, distinguished from those which concern our enquiry? Certainly not by the first sort being *secret*. For the first sort are often not secret, and in some cultures are barely meant to be so, it being an achievement calling for admiration that one has stolen extensively and conspicuously from the public funds. Even more obviously, many dubious acts of the more strictly political kind are themselves secret. The point rather is that not all acts done by politicians are political acts, and we are concerned with those that are. Relative to some appropriate account of what the politician is supposed to be up to as a politician, stealing from public funds is likely to count as a diversion of effort. However, it is to be recognized that not all classifications which would be made on these principles by the most respectable north-west European or North American opinion would come out the same elsewhere; thus bribery can be an integral and functional part of a political system. What must count as a political activity anywhere, however, is *trying to stay in office.* There are, needless to say, unacceptable ways of staying in office, and there are among them ways of staying in office which defeat the purposes of the methods for acquiring office (rigging the ballot). But this is a matter of means – the *objective* of staying in office, though it cannot by every means or in every circumstance be decently attained, is itself highly relevant to the business of politics, whereas the objectives of enriching oneself or of securing sinecures for one's family are not.

We shall leave aside the dubious activities of politicians which are not primarily political activities. But since the question we shall be concerned with is primarily what dispositions we want in politicians, we should not at the same time forget the platitude that the psychological distance between the two sorts of activity may be very small indeed. Not every politically ruthless or devious ruler is disposed to enrich himself or improperly advance his friends (the ones who are not are usually morally and psychologically more interesting). But the two sorts of tendency go together often enough, and cries for 'clean government' are usually demands for the suppression of both.

There is another aspect of the subject that I shall mention only in passing. I shall consider the politician as the originator of action, or at least as a joint originator of action, rather than as one who participates in a party or government, or acquiesces, with respect to decisions which he does not help to make. Some of the issues we shall consider apply to those who originate at any level; other larger issues apply only to those who originate at some higher level, such as a President or Prime Minister or (in the British system) a Cabinet Minister. This emphasis leaves on one side the question of a politician's responsibility, and hence the view one should take of him, when he agrees with a measure but did not originate it. It also leaves aside the more interesting question of his responsibility when he does not agree with it but acquiesces in it or stays in a position where he is identified with it – what is, in a democratic system at least, the *resigning problem*.

One remark is perhaps worth making here in relation to that problem. Resigning, or again refraining from resigning, cannot be straightforwardly either instrumental or expressive acts. Instrumental considerations of course bear on the issue, as in the classical 'working from within' argument which has kept many queasy people tied to many appalling ventures for remarkably long periods. Yet such decisions cannot, in the nature of the case, be purely and in all cases instrumental, since the decision has a class of consequences which themselves depend on the agent's being perceived as not being entirely consequentialist about it. Among the consequences of the act are some that depend on what it is taken to mean, so that the purely consequentialist agent would be faced, if he fully considered the consequences, with the fact that what he is doing is by its nature something which cannot be adequately thought about purely in terms of its consequences. On the other hand, to view resignation as the mere equivalent of saying 'I agree' or 'I disagree' in a private and uncoerced conversation would be an elementary misunderstanding, entertained only by someone who neglected the difference between a commitment to ongoing political activity, and a one-off example of political expression. It is also, therefore, to neglect the point that for a politician such a decision is, in a substantial and relevant sense, part of his life.

When that point is seen, moreover, it is often seen in the wrong terms – it naturally invites being seen in the wrong terms. For a career politician, resignation is likely to affect the relation of his life to politics altogether. He must consider the decision to resign in the context of a commitment to a political life, and that can of course be read as his attending to his career. No doubt it is true of some in this situation that they are simply attending to their career, but it is important, both for the public and for the politician, to recognize that there is a structural reason why it should be difficult to tell whether that is true or not.

Among political acts are some for which there are good political reasons, as that important and worthy political projects would fail without these acts, but which are acts that honourable and scrupulous people might, *prima facie* at least, be disinclined to do. Besides those, there are more, and more insidious, cases in which the unpalatable act seems necessary not to achieve any such clear-cut and noble objective, but just to keep going, or to pre-empt opposition to a worthy project, or more generally to prevent a worthy project becoming impossible later. What the unpalatable acts may be depends on the political environment. At this stage we are concerned with a relatively ordered situation where political activity involves at least bargaining and the expression of conflicting interests and ideals. In such a situation a politician might find himself involved in, or invited to, such things as lying, or at least concealment and the making of misleading statements; breaking promises; special pleading; temporary coalition with the distasteful; sacrifice of the interests of worthy persons to those of unworthy persons; and (at least if in a sufficiently important position) coercion up to blackmail. We are not at this point considering more drastic situations in which there is a question, for instance, of having opponents killed. (I mean by that, that *there is no question of it*, and it would be thought outrageous or insane to mention it as an option. The situation is not one of those in which such options are mentioned and then, all things considered, laid aside.)

The less drastic, but still morally distasteful, activities are in no way confined to politics. That they should seem necessary follows just from there being large interests involved, in a context of partly unstructured bargaining. It is the same, for instance, with a lot of business of the more active variety. But it attracts more obloquy in politics than elsewhere; the use of such means is thought more appropriate to the pursuit of professedly self-interested ends than where larger moral pretensions are entertained. But the fact that there are larger moral pretensions is itself not an accident. Besides the point that some objectives other than the self-interest of the professional participants are necessary — at the limit, are necessary for the activity even to be politics — there is the point that democracy has a tendency to impose higher expectations with regard even to the means, since under democracy control of politicians is precisely supposed to be a function of the expectations of the electorate.

I have mentioned acts, done in pursuit of worthy political ends, which 'honourable and scrupulous people might, *prima facie* at least, be disinclined to do'. But, it will be said, if it is for some worthy political objective and the greater good, does not that merely show that it is an act which these honourable people should *not* be disinclined to do? At most, the characteristic which the act possesses is that it is of a type which these people would be disinclined to do if it were not in this interest, and that, it may be said, is irrelevant. But this Utilitarian response either does not get to the question which concerns us, or else gives an inadequate answer to it. It does not get to the question if it merely insists that the otherwise discreditable act is the one, in these circumstances, to be done, and says nothing about the dispositions of the agent and how those dispositions express themselves in a view of this act. It gives an inadequate answer if it says that the only disposition such an agent needs is the disposition to do what is Utilitarianly right. Even Utilitarians have found that answer inadequate. It is not self-evident, and many Utilitarians agree that it is not even true, that the best way to secure their objective of the greatest happiness all round is to have agents each of whom is pursuing, as such, the greatest happiness all round. Beyond that level of discussion, again, there is the deeper point that moral dispositions other than Utilitarian benevolence may themselves figure in people's conceptions of 'happiness'.

In any case, it is not enough to say that these are situations in which the right thing to do is an act which would *normally* be morally objectionable. This description best fits the case in which an act and its situation constitute an *exception*. We may recall the repertoire, familiar from Ross and other writers, of obligations properly overridden in emergencies. There, the decision is often easy – of course we break the routine promise to save the drowning child, and to doubt it, or to feel uneasy about having done it, would be utterly unreasonable. It is a clear overriding circumstance. While it is not as though the promise or other defeated obligation had never existed (one still has the obligation at least to explain), nevertheless it is quite clearly and unanswerably overridden, and complaints from the disadvantaged party would, once things had been explained, be unacceptable. Of course, not all cases of the straight overriding kind are clear cases of that kind. One can be in doubt what to do, and here there is room for unease. But the unease, within this structure, is directly related to the doubt or unclarity: the question will be 'did I really do the right thing?'. If one has an uneasy sense that one may have done wrong to the victim, it is because one has an uneasy sense that one may have done the wrong thing.

Some situations in politics are no doubt of that structure. But the situations I have in mind (of course, as I have said, they are not confined to politics) are of a different structure. In these, the sense that a discreditable thing has been done is not the product of uncertainty,

nor again of a recognition that one has made the wrong choice. A sense
that something discreditable has been done will, moreover, be properly
shared by the victims, and they will have a complaint that they have
been wronged. The politician who just could not see that they had
a complaint, and who, after he had explained the situation to them,
genuinely thought that their complaint was based on a misunderstanding
and that they were unreasonable to make it (as one might properly
think in the first kind of case) is a politician whose dispositions are
already such as to raise our questions in a very pressing form.

I do not have in mind here drastic cases of tragic choice, where one
might say that whatever the agent did was wrong.[1] They, though not
merely exceptions, are certainly exceptional. The cases we are
considering are not just what our normal categories count as exceptions,
nor are they of the exceptional kind that reaches beyond our normal
categories. Nor, again, need the decision be at all uncertain. It will often
be true of these cases that so long as the agent takes seriously the moral
frames of reference or reasons which support each of the courses of
action, it will be clear what he should do. But the clarity in such a
case is not that of the vivid emergency exception, nor is it the clarity
of the impossible, which can attend the tragic case. It is clear because
it is everyday, part of the business: not too often part of the business,
one hopes, but part of the business all the same. If the politician is going
to take the claims of politics seriously, including the moral claims of
politics, and if he is going to act at anything except a modest and largely
administrative level of responsibility, then he has to face at least the
probability of situations of this kind. If he shares the highest
responsibilities, it is virtually concern that he will encounter them.
Below that level, he may perhaps not. He may operate in a very docile
and citizenly environment. He may be lucky. He may even have, as
a few seem to have, a virtue or moral cunning which drives such
situations away. But it is a predictable and probable hazard of public
life that there will be these situations in which something morally
disagreeable is clearly required. To refuse on moral grounds ever to
do anything of that sort is more than likely to mean that one cannot
seriously pursue even the moral ends of politics.

Yet, at the same time, the moral disagreeableness of these acts is not
merely cancelled, and this comes out above all in the consideration that
the victims can justly complain that they have been wronged. It is

[1] I have said something about such cases in 'Ethical Consistency', in *Problems of the
Self* (Cambridge 1973), ch. 11.

undeniable, for instance, that the agent has lied, or deliberately misled them, or bullied them, or let them down, or used them. It may be that when it is all explained, they understand, but it is foolish to say, even then, that they have no right to complain.

It may be said that the victims do not have a right to complain because their relation to the action is not the same in the political context as it would be outside it. Perhaps it is not even the same action. There is some truth, sometimes, in this claim. It does apply to some victims themselves involved in politics: a certain level of roughness is to be expected by anyone who understands the nature of the activity, and it is merely a misunderstanding to go on about it in a way which might be appropriate to more sheltered activities. But this consideration – which might be called *Truman's kitchen-heat principle* – does not go all the way. There are victims outside politics, and there are victims inside it who get worse than they could reasonably expect, and in general there are political acts which no considerations about appropriate expectations or the going currency of the trade can in themselves adequately excuse.

I mentioned the 'moral claims' of politics. In some cases the claims of the political reasons are proximate enough, and enough of the moral kind, to enable one to say that there is a moral justification for that particular political act, a justification which has outweighed the moral reasons against it. Even so, that can still leave the moral remainder, the uncancelled moral disagreeableness I have referred to. The possibility of such a remainder is not peculiar to political action, but there are features of politics which make it specially liable to produce it. It particularly arises in cases where the moral justification of the action is of a consequentialist or maximizing kind, while what has gone to the wall is a right. There is a larger moral cost attached to letting a right be overridden by consequences, than to letting one consequence be overridden by another, since it is part of the point of rights that they cannot just[2] be overridden by consequences. In politics the justifying consideration will characteristically be of the consequentialist kind. Moreover, an important aspect of consequentialist reasoning lies in maximizing *expectation*, the product of the size of the pay-off and its probability. Since in the political sphere of action the pay-offs are,

[2] I assume that rights can sometimes be overridden. To define 'rights' so that this should not ever be possible would have wider consequences – since one must say something about possible conflicts of rights among themselves – and is anyway undesirable: if all rights have to be *absolute* rights, then it is plausible to conclude that there are no rights at all.

or can readily be thought to be, very large, the probabilities can be quite small, and the victims may find that their rights have been violated for the sake of an outside chance.

Where the political reasons are of the less proximate kind, for instance defensive, or pre-emptive, or concerned with securing an opportunity, we may speak, not of the moral claims of politics, but merely of the claims of politics against morality. While an anxious politician may hope still to find some moral considerations bearing on the situation, he may discover that they have retreated merely to the overall justification of the pursuit of his, or his party's, worthwhile objectives, or some similar over-arching concern. The Olympian point of retreat is notoriously so distant and invulnerable that the rationale of seriously[3] carrying on the business of politics ceases to be disturbed by any moral qualms or any sense of non-political costs at all. Decent political existence lies somewhere between that – or its totally cynical successor, from which even the distant view of Olympus has disappeared – and an absurd failure to recognize that if politics is to exist as an activity at all, some moral considerations must be expected to get out of its way.

If that space is to have any hope of being occupied, we need to hold on to the idea, and to find some politicians who will hold on to the idea, that there are actions which remain morally disagreeable even when politically justified. The point of this is not at all that it is edifying to have politicians who, while as ruthless in action as others, are unhappy about it. Sackcloth is not suitable dress for politicians, least of all successful ones. The point – and this is basic to my argument – is that only those who are reluctant or disinclined to do the morally disagreeable when it is really necessary have much chance of not doing it when it is not necessary.

There are two different reasons for this. First, there is no disposition which just consists in getting it right every time, whether in politics or in anything else. Whether judgment is well exercised, whether immediate moral objections are given the right weight, or any, against large long-term issues, is, on any sensible view of those processes, something that involves patterns of sentiment and reaction. In a body of persons considering a practical question, it essentially involves their

---

[3] I have known a politician, now dead, who used to say 'that is not a *serious* political argument' to mean, more or less, 'that is an argument about what to do in politics which mentions a non-political consideration' – in particular, a moral consideration. This posture was to some degree bluff.

shared dispositions and their mutual expectations – what considerations can be heard, what kinds of hesitation or qualification or obstacle it is appropriate or effective to mention. (There is a remark attributed to Keynes, about an American official: 'a man who has his ear so close to the ground that he cannot hear what an upright man says'.) That is the first, and main, reason, and one which any reasonable view of deliberation must accept: a habit of reluctance is an essential obstacle against the happy acceptance of the intolerable.

The second reason, which I have already included in my account, is something less widely acceptable: that reluctance in the necessary case, is not only a useful habit, but a correct reaction *to that case*, because that case does involve a genuine moral cost. The fact that reluctance is justified even in the necessary case – and in speaking of 'reluctance', I mean not just initial hesitation in reaching for the answer, but genuine disquiet when one arrives at it – is in fact something that helps to explain the nature, and the value, of the habit of reluctance which was appealed to in the first reason. It embodies a sensibility to moral costs. Utilitarianism, which hopes (in some of its indirect forms) to appeal to habits of reluctance, cannot in fact make any sense of them at this level, because it lacks any sense of *moral* cost, as opposed to costs of some other kind (such as utility) which have to be considered in arriving at the moral decision. Utilitarianism has its special reasons for not understanding the notion of a moral cost, which are connected with its maximising conceptions, but much other moral philosophy shares that incapacity. Yet it is a notion deeply entrenched in many people's moral consciousness. Why so many moral philosophers learn to forget it is a harder question, and perhaps a deeper one, than why some politicians do.

If then, there can be agents who in this way have good moral reason to do things which they have good reason to think are, and remain, morally distasteful, a way of understanding their situation might be to see it as one in which the agent has some special relationship to parties involved, which will give him an honourable motive for overruling his objections to such acts. This is the model which Charles Fried in a recent paper ('The Lawyer as Friend: The Moral Foundations of the Lawyer–Client Relation', 85 *Yale Law Journal* (1976), pp. 1060–89) has applied to the case (in some ways similar) of the lawyer who is required on behalf of his client to do things one would not feel morally well-disposed towards doing, such as harassing witnesses or pressing a formal advantage of well-off persons against the vital interests of less well-off persons. Fried invokes in this connexion the relationship of friendship, modelling the lawyer's relationship to his client on the kind of personal relationship which would be widely acknowledged to permit or even require departures from what would otherwise be the demands of impartiality. Fried honestly raises and confronts the problem, but it is hard to be convinced by the model that he has brought to bear on it. For one thing – a point which he mentions but, it seems to me, does not dispose of – one is not paid to be someone's friend; for another, the honourable man who is in question might not be expected to have friends who are like some of the lawyer's clients, or who expect him to do what some of the lawyer's clients expect him to do.

There are some analogies to a special relationship model in politics, inasmuch as politics involves loyalties or allegiances which require one to be something other than impartial. But while there are some allegiances of this kind, to country or party or electorate, and they play some role, they are not adequate, any more than a personal relationship to the client in the legal case, to cover the full range of these issues. Rather, the legal case very readily presses on us a different sort of question which is not only a useful question to ask but also, I think, *the* useful question to ask in these connexions: what sort of system does one want, and what sort of disposition does one want in the person acting? We then have to think about how the answers to these questions can be harmonised, in the light of the question: what dispositions does the system require or favour?

The example of the law raises some interesting questions in this connexion, and I shall pursue it a little further. One has to ask how the desired product of legal activity, justice, is related to an adversarial system, and to what extent the sorts of behaviour that concern Fried are encouraged or required by such a system. That is, in fact, only the start of the problem, for if the adversarial system succeeds in producing justice, one factor in that must be the presence of a judge – and judges are lawyers, and usually former advocates. The judicial disposition is not the same as the adversarial disposition, but as our system of recruitment for judges works, the one has somehow to issue from the other.

Let us, however, stick to the adversarial case. Concentrating on the morally disagreeable activities which may be involved in the enforcement of some legal rights (e.g. some legal rights of the strong against the weak), we may be tempted by the following argument.

(1) In any complex society (at least) the enforcement of some legal rights involves morally disagreeable acts.

(2) It is bad that legal rights which exist should not be enforceable.

(3) Enforcement of many rights of the kind mentioned in (1) requires lawyers.

(4) Any lawyer really effective in enforcing those rights must be fairly horrible.

ERGO (5) It is good that some lawyers are fairly horrible.

How might this argument be met, if at all? The conventional answer presumably lies in denying (1), but in our context of discussion, we will not accept as sufficient the conventional reason for denying it, namely that there is a sufficient moral justification for the system that requires those acts (which is in effect equivalent to (2)). Another line would be to deny (2). This is perhaps the approach of Wasserstrom,[4] who inclines to the view that if (1) carries much weight with regard to some rights, then it may just be better that those rights be not enforced. If this goes beyond the position of refusing to act when one knows that someone else will (not necessarily an objectionable position), it runs into difficulties about the operation of the law as a roughly predictable system. Fried denies (4), by putting the acts required in (1) into the framework of loyalty and friendship. Others might combat (4) by using notions of professionalism, insisting that since those acts are done in a professional role, in the name of a desirable system, it cannot follow that they express a horrible disposition – they are not, in that sense, personal acts at all.

The phenomenology of the states of mind invoked by that answer is very complex. The limitations of the answer are, however, fairly obvious and indeed notorious. One limitation, for instance, must lie in the consideration that it is a personal fact about somebody that that is his profession. However, whatever we think in general about those ideas of professionalism, there is at least one thing that can be allowed to the lawyer's situation which it is hard to allow to the politician's. Even if we accepted (5), the disagreeable conclusion of the argument, we could at least agree that the professional activities of lawyers are delimited enough to make it a matter of limited account to the public

[4] 'Lawyers as Professionals: some moral issues', *Human Rights*, vol. 5 (1975), pp. 2–24. I am grateful for discussion of these issues to Dick Wasserstrom, Andy Kaufman, and other participants in the Council for Philosophical Studies Institute on Law and Ethics, Williams College, Mass., 1977.

that some lawyers are fairly horrible. The ways in which the argument, if sound, shows them to be horrible are ways which their clients, at any rate, have no reason to regret. But there is much less reason for such comfort in the politicians' case, and if a comparable argument can be mounted with them, then the public has reason to be alarmed. The professional sphere of activity is very much less delimited, and there are important asymmetries, for example in the matter of concealment. The line between the client and the other side is one which in an adversarial system governs a great deal of the lawyer's behaviour, and certainly the sorts of reasons he has for concealing things from the opposition are not characteristically reasons for concealment from his client. But the reasons there are for concealing things in politics are always reasons for concealing them from the electorate.

Another reason for concern in the political case lies in the professional (and in itself perfectly proper) commitment to staying in power. I have already suggested that it involves an essential ambivalence: it is impossible to tell, at the limit, where it merges into simple ambition, and into that particular deformation of political life, under all systems, which consists in the inability to consider a question on its merits because one's attention is directed to the consequences of giving (to one's colleagues, in the first instance) a particular answer. Where that had widely taken over, the citizens have reason to fear their politicians' judgment.

The dispositions of politicians are differently related to their tasks and to their public than are those of a profession such as the legal profession for which partly analogous questions arise. Those differences all give greater reason for concern, and make more pressing the question: what features of the political system are likely to select for those dispositions in politicians which are at once morally welcome and compatible with their being effective politicians? What features of the system can help to bring it about that fairly decent people can dispose of a fair degree of power? How does one ensure a reasonable succession of colonists of the space between cynicism and political idiocy?

It is a vast, old, and in good part empirical question. If one adapts Plato's question, *how can the good rule?*, to Machiavelli's, *how to rule the world as it is?*, the simplest conflation – *how can the good rule the world as it is?* – is merely discouraging. It is also, however, excessively pious. The conception of the good that it inherits from Plato invites the question of how the good could do anything at all, while the Machiavellian conception of the world as it is raises the question of how anyone could do anything with it. (A popular sense of 'realism' gets its strength from the fact that the second of those questions has some answers, while the first has none.) But if one modifies from both ends, allowing that the good need not be as pure as all that, so long as they retain some active sense of moral costs and moral limits, and that the society has some genuinely settled politics and some expectations of civic respectability, then there is some place for discussing what properties we should like the system, in these respects, to have. There are many: I will mention, only in barest outline, four dimensions of a political system which seem to bear closely on this issue.

(a) There is the question, already touched on, of the balance of publicity, and the relations of politician and public, particularly of course in a democracy. The assumption is widespread, particularly in the USA, that public government and a great deal of public scrutiny must encourage honest government, and apply controls to the cynicism of politicians. There is, however, no reason to suppose that the influence of such practices and institutions will be uniformly in one direction. The requirements of instant publicity in a context which is, as we are supposing, to some mild degree moralised, has an evident potential for hypocrisy, while, even apart from that, the instant identification of particular political acts, as they are represented at the degree of resolution achievable in the media, is a recipe for competition in pre-emptive press releases.

(b) A similar question is that of the relations of politicians to one another; and there is another approved belief, that it is in the interest of good government that politicians should basically be related to one another only functionally, that they should not share a set of understandings which too markedly differentiate them from people who are not politicians. Yet it is not clear how far this is true, either. It is an important function of the relations of politicians to one another, what courses of action are even discussible, and that is a basic dimension of a moral culture. Very obviously, a ruthless clique is worse than a clique checked by less ruthless outsiders, but that is not the only option. Another is that of a less ruthless clique resisting more ruthless outsiders.

(c) A very well-known point is that of the relation of potential politicians to actual ones, the question of political recruitment. Notoriously, systems where succession is problematic or discontinuous have the property of selecting for the ruthless. No sensible critic will suggest that if that is so, it is at all easy to change, but it is nevertheless an important dimension of assessment of a political system.

(d) A slightly less obvious variant of the same sort of issue concerns the promotion-pattern within a political organization: in particular, the position of the bottleneck between very top jobs and rather less top jobs. Except in very favoured circumstances, it is likely to be the case that getting to the top of a political system will require properties which, while they need not at all necessarily be spectacularly undesirable or even regrettable, may nevertheless lean in the direction of the kind of ambition and professionalism which does not always make for the best judgment, moral or practical. It is desirable that the system should not put too heavy stress on those properties too soon in the business; there can then be an honourable and successful role, below the final bottleneck, for persons without the elbow-power to get into or through the bottleneck. Government concentrated on a few personalities of course tends to weaken this possibility. Related is the question of the prestige of jobs below the top one. It was a notable fact, remarked by some commentators, that when the English politician R. A. (now Lord) Butler retired from politics, it was suggested that his career had been a failure because – and although – he had held almost every major office of state except the Premiership itself.

These are, of course, only hints at certain dimensions of discussion. The aim is just to suggest that it is such ways that one should think about the disagreeable acts involved in (everyday) politics – that fruitful thought should be directed to the aspects of a political system which may make it less likely that the only persons attracted to a profession which undoubtedly involves some such acts will be persons who are insufficiently disposed to find them disagreeable.

Last, I should like to make just one point about the further dimension of the subject, in which one is concerned not just with the disagreeable or distasteful but with crimes, or what otherwise would be crimes. This is a different level from the last: here we are concerned not just with business but, so to speak, with the Mafia. My question, rather as before, is not directly whether actions of a certain kind – in this case such things as murders, torture, etc. – are ever justified, but rather, if they are justified, how we should think of those who politically bring them about. I shall call the actions in question, for short, *violence*. It might be worth distinguishing, among official acts of violence, what could be called *structured* and *unstructured* violence. The former relate to such processes as executions under law, application of legal force by the police, etc., while the latter include acts (it may be, more abroad than at home) pursued in what is regarded as the national interest.

I shall set out a list of four propositions which some would regard as all true, and which, if they were all true, would make the hope of finding politicians of honourable character, except in minor roles and in favourable circumstances, very slim.

(i) There are violent acts which the state is justified in doing which no private citizen as such would be justified in doing.

(ii) Anything the state is justified in doing, some official such as, often, a politician is justified in ordering to be done.

(iii) You are not morally justified in ordering to be done anything which you would not be prepared to do yourself.

(iv) Official violence is enough like unofficial violence for the preparedness referred to in (iii) to amount to a criminal tendency.

I take it that no-one except anarchists will deny (i), at least so far as structured violence is concerned (it is admitted that the distinction between structured and unstructured violence is imprecise). It may be said that structured violence constitutes acts which none but the state could even logically perform: thus nothing done by a private citizen as such could constitute a judicial execution. But I take it that while this is true, it does not cut very deep into the essential issues – there is another description of the act which is a judicial execution under which that act could logically, but ought not to be, performed by a private citizen. A more substantial issue is whether the only violence that is legitimate for the state is structured violence. This I doubt, too. Even if regular military operations are counted as structured violence, there may be other acts, bordering on the military or of an irregular character, which a state may be lucky if it is in a position to do without altogether.

An important issue connected with this is the extent to which a political leader's task, particularly in a democracy, is defined in terms of defending the interests of the state; and whether, if the interests of some other, rival, state will be advanced unless some act of violence is authorized, he can be justified in refusing to authorize that act. A similar problem arises in the case where he thinks that the interests of another state should, in justice, prevail. He certainly has a right to that opinion; to what extent has he the right to act on it while still performing that role?

The (imprecise) distinction between structured and unstructured violence also bears on (iv). (iv) is perhaps more plausible with un-structured than with structured violence. It is very widely agreed that the distinction between the official and the unofficial can make a moral difference to the estimation of acts of violence; there are similarly psychological differences in the dispositions underlying the two kinds of acts, even if it is unclear how deep those differences may, in many cases, go (an unclarity which itself makes some people unduly nervous about the legitimacy of official violence). If that is right, then (iv) will fail, and the disobliging conclusion will not follow from the argument, even granted the truth of (i) and the platitudinous truth of (ii). At least, it will be enough to prevent its following with full generality. But while we may certainly agree that (iv) is not exceptionlessly true, it is quite plausible to claim that there are acts, particularly perhaps of unstructured violence, for which (iv) really does hold true, but which nevertheless would be justified under (i). To suppose that there could be no such acts, to suppose in particular that if an act is such that (iv) applies to it, then it must follow that it could not be justified, would be, it seems to me, to take a highly unrealistic view either of politics, or of the possible psychology of agents who will do that act.

In this case, attention turns to (iii); (iii) seems to me false, and more interestingly so than (iv). If so, then there is perhaps a larger class of arguments which have some currency in moral discussion which will have to be abandoned or given extra help, as that one should be a vegetarian unless one would be prepared to work in an abattoir, or that one should not accept experimentation on animals unless one were prepared to conduct it (assuming that one had the skills) oneself. However it may be with those cases, at any rate our understanding of honesty and decency in politicians should be modified by reflexion on (iii). The consideration that they should not order something unless they were prepared to do it themselves should be counterweighted with the consideration that if they were prepared to do it themselves, they might be far too willing to order it.

5　Conflicts of values

Isaiah Berlin has always insisted that there is a plurality of values which can conflict with one another, and which are not reducible to one another; consequently, that we cannot conceive of a situation in which it was true both that all value-conflict had been eliminated, and that there had been no loss of value on the way. To have insisted on these truths is one of the conspicuous services that Berlin has rendered to a sound and humane conception of social thought.

In Berlin's own thought, these truths are associated with the foundations of liberalism.[1] The history of that movement itself shows that the consequences of these views need not be quietist or conservative. Yet while this has been so, there does remain a problem about the relation of this kind of pluralism to action, a problem at least for a modern, developed, and relatively liberal society. Even there, it is of course true that the business of reaffirming and defending the plurality of values is itself a political task, one to which Berlin's writings make a permanent contribution. But more is needed, if the pluralist is not to spend too much of his time as a rueful spectator of political change which is itself powered by forces which either have nothing to do with values at all, or else express value-claims more exclusive than the pluralist himself would admit.

There does not exist much adequate philosophy on the question of how a pluralistic theory of values might be combined with, indeed issue in, radical social action. The conditions of there being any such philosophy are certainly complex and at present unclear. But we shall be able to see how, if at all, they might be satisfied only if we understand better than we do now what it is for values to be plural, conflicting and irreducible. That means understanding, in particular, their conflicts, since it is precisely their conflicts which systematisers

---

[1] I have speculated about the form of that association in my introduction to Berlin's collection of philosophical papers, *Concepts and Categories* (London, 1978).

(at the limit, reductionists) seek to overcome, while pluralists of the Berlin spirit regard the conflicts as both ineliminable and not resoluble without remainder. These remarks will be concerned with the subject of conflict.

It is in fact a large subject – larger than might be suggested by the literature, which has typically tended to regard value-conflict, except perhaps in the most contingent and superficial connections, as a pathology of social and moral thought, and as something to be overcome, whether by theorising, as in the tradition of analytical philosophy and its ancestors, or by an historical process, as in Hegelian and Marxist interpretations. It is my view, as it is Berlin's, that value-conflict is not necessarily pathological at all, but something necessarily involved in human values, and to be taken as central by an adequate understanding of them. I also think, though Berlin may not, that where conflict needs to be overcome, this 'need' is not of a purely logical character, nor a requirement of pure rationality, but rather a kind of social or personal need, the pressure of which will be felt in some historical circumstances rather than others.

The type of conflict that will concern us is one-party conflict; and we will take that as one-*person* conflict. (There are of course one-party conflicts where the party is not one person, as with policy disagreements within a firm or other such agency, but for present purposes these can be regarded as special cases of two- (or more) party conflict in the context of agreed procedures or objectives.) Philosophical inquiry which is primarily concerned with epistemological or semantic issues of objectivity naturally concentrates on two-party conflict, where the problem is that of resolving *disagreement*, and it is assumed that the parties have each their own harmonious set of value-beliefs. Accompanying that, usually, is an assumption that, whatever may turn out to be the case with two-party conflicts, at any rate one-person conflict must be capable of being rationally resolved. At the very least, the theory of rational behaviour must make it an undisputed aim of the rational agent to reduce conflict in his personal set of values to the minimum. This assumption is characteristically made even by those who do not think that interpersonal conflicts of value necessarily admit of rational resolution.

The assumption is in fact unreasonable. For those, moreover, who combine it with scepticism about rationally resolving interpersonal conflict, it is doubly unreasonable, since some one-person conflicts of values are expressions of a complex inheritance of values, from different social sources, and what we experience in ourselves as a conflict is something which could have been, and perhaps was, expressed as a conflict between two societies, or between two historical states of one society. The same point also comes out in the opposite direction. A characteristic dispute about values in society, such as some issue of equality against freedom, is not one most typically enacted by a body of single-minded egalitarians confronting a body of equally single-minded libertarians, but is rather a conflict which one person, equipped with a more generous range of human values, could find enacted in himself.

It is worth taking first, if briefly, the type of one-person conflict which has in fact been most studied – the so-called conflict of obligations. This is the area of the conflict of values which is most directly linked to reasons for action. As such, it is not entirely typical, but it does present some useful considerations. In particular, it reveals some ways in which conflict is not necessarily pathological, even though it is real conflict and both the obligations which are parties to the conflict actually exist and actually apply to the situation.

Such cases are basically different from those others, themselves very familiar, in which conflict is only apparent, and there are not in fact two conflicting obligations at all. For example, suppose an agent promises his father to support, after the father's death, a certain charity, but he later finds himself short of money and cannot both support the charity and, let us say, make some provision for his own children which he feels he should make. One resolution of the problem which could be available is that he had reason in good faith to think that it was a tacit but understood condition on the promise that it applied only if there were enough money left after such things as providing for his children. Whether this thought was sound would of course be a matter of historical fact and judgement – it would not become sound just because it resolved the difficulty. But if it is sound, then there is no conflict at all. One of the obligations has evaporated.

There is a temptation, helped by the ambiguous terminology of 'prima facie obligations', to take this relatively painless kind of case as the pattern for the resolution of a conflict of obligations. The evident fact that there is at most one of the two things which, all things considered, I should do, is taken to be equivalent to the idea that, all things considered, there is only one obligation. But this is a mistake. There are certainly two obligations in a real case of this kind, though one may outweigh the other. The one that outweighs has greater stringency, but the one that is outweighed also possesses some stringency, and this is expressed in what, by way of compensation, I may have to do for the parties who are disadvantaged by its being outweighed; whether I have merely to explain and apologise, or whether I have to engage further in some more substantial reparatory action. (Those who rely heavily on 'ought implies can' in these connections should consider why – particularly if the conflict of obligations was not my fault – I should have to do any of these things.) The fact, on the other hand, that one obligation was genuinely outweighed by the other is expressed in the consideration that the disadvantaged party has no justified complaint about what I chose to do. They may have some complaint about my compensatory activity, or lack of it, but if the obligation was indeed outweighed, then they have no justified complaint about my not having done what I was obliged to them to do, except perhaps to the extent that the conflict of obligations was my own fault.

In another, and more drastic, kind of case, however,[2] which might be called the 'tragic' kind, an agent can justifiably think that whatever he does will be wrong: that there are conflicting moral requirements, and that neither of them succeeds in overriding or outweighing the other. In this case, though it can actually emerge from deliberation that one of the courses of action is the one that, all things considered, one had better take, it is, and it remains, true that each of the courses of action is morally required, and at a level which means that, whatever he does, the agent will have reason to feel regret at the deepest level. If, in such a case, we do not necessarily say that the victims have a justified complaint, it is because such cases can lie beyond complaint, as they can lie also beyond any adequate compensatory action.

I shall not raise here any questions of detail about the logic of such situations.[3] The present point is that it must be a mistake to suppose that what we have here is a case of logical inconsistency, such that the agent could not be justified or rational in thinking that each of these moral requirements applied to him. This is to misplace the source of the agent's trouble, in suggesting that what is wrong is his thought about the moral situation, whereas what is wrong lies in his situation

---

[2] There are further cases: e.g. a political type of case, which is not exceptional, as the tragic case is, but where, unlike the situation of outweighing, the victim has a justified complaint. See chapter 4 above, pp. 58 seqq.

[3] I have discussed some of them in 'Ethical Consistency', in *Problems of the Self* (Cambridge, 1973). The central notion of agent-regret is considered in chapter 2, above.

itself – something which may or may not be his fault. Someone might argue on larger metaphysical grounds that it was impossible that any agent should meet such a situation; but, if there were such an argument, it would have to yield a metaphysical impossibility, or, in some way, a moral impossibility, and not a proof that the judgements involved in such a situation were contradictory. There is a substantial and interesting question: 'What would have to be true of the world and of an agent that it should be impossible for him to be in a situation where whatever he did was wrong?' I doubt in fact that there is anything that could produce such a guarantee short of the existence of a rather interventionist God, or else the total reduction of moral life to rules of efficient behaviour – two extremes which precisely leave out the actual location of moral experience. But it is at any rate a real question, and it would not be a real question if the correct thing to say were that nothing has to be true of the agent or of the world for this to be so, because it is guaranteed by the logic of moral expressions.

In this, as elsewhere in these areas, logical and semantic theory has to be responsive to experience, and to what a reflective agent feels that he needs to say. At the same time, it is of course true that such experiences need interpretation in terms of general ideas about the status of moral thought – for instance, with regard to issues of objectivity. It is notable that insofar as it is features of our moral experience that draw us towards ideas of the objectivity of ethics, the experience of moral conflict is precisely one that conveys most strongly such an idea. That there is nothing that one decently, honourably, or adequately *can* do seems a kind of truth as firmly independent of the will and inclination as anything in morality. Indeed it is independent of the will and inclination, but it does not follow that it is independent of what one is, nor that these impressions represent an order of things independent of oneself.

Conflicts of obligation are peculiar in presenting a conflict between determinately specified actions, while the tragic ones among them are further peculiar in lying beyond the ordinary routes of moral thought. Very many of our conflicts, however, including those that have most interested Berlin, are at a level where interpretation in action is less determinate or immediate. Values such as liberty, equality, and expressions of justice other than equality, can certainly conflict as ideals or objectives, though their connection with immediately presented courses of action may often be problematical, while, in the other direction, a choice between presented courses of action may in some cases be only indeterminately guided or shaped by appeal to these values.[4]

Still further from particular choices of action or policy are evaluations of admirable human characteristics or virtues such as courage, gentleness, honesty, independence of spirit and so forth. We know, too, that no social institution or form of society can express, embody or encourage all of them equally. One form of Utopianism — the basic form, perhaps — consists in supposing that a society could be attained in which all genuinely valuable human characteristics could be equally and harmoniously displayed. Since it is obvious that not every characteristic which has been accepted in the course of history as a virtue could be so combined, some opinions about what are virtues have to be dismissed. By the more sophisticated Utopians, they are dismissed as forms of false consciousness, which are revealed as false by the same reflections as yield the structure of Utopia. An easy — too easy — example is working-class deference.

That example, and others, will remind us that a critique of supposed virtues must be possible, and it should be an aim of a developed moral and social philosophy to provide one. Yet, even granted such a critique, there is little substance to the Utopian hope. Those who share Berlin's scepticism about that hope — and perhaps also some of his fears about attempts to enact it — will think that while society can move to recognise and express new virtues and ideals, perhaps even a wider range of them, nevertheless there are at the same time irrecoverable losses. As in a given choice at a given time one value has to be set against another, so also there is loss of genuine human value over time.

There is a further proposition which some of these will believe (among them, I believe, Berlin): that there is no common currency in which these gains and losses of value can be computed, that values, or at least the most basic values, are not only plural but in a real sense incommensurable. Some other people, however, sympathetic to the general drift of the argument so far, may at this point protest. To say that values necessarily conflict, and that the affirmation of some necessarily involves losses with regard to others, does not entail that they are incommensurable. The reference to *losses* does not in itself entail, on the other hand, that they are commensurable: one could register a loss in one dimension of value without comparing the amount

---

[4] One of the several simplifying comforts offered by the purely transactional account of distributive justice which is given by Robert Nozick is that it firmly reduces this dimension of indeterminacy.

of that loss with another dimension of value. But unless some comparison can be made, then nothing rational can be said at all about what overall outcome is to be preferred, nor about which side of a conflict is to be chosen – and that is certainly a despairing conclusion. *Some* overall comparisons can be made, and if they can, then to some degree, it will be said, these values must be commensurable.

The objection can be pressed further. When it is said that values are incommensurable, it is usually some general values such as liberty and equality that are said to be incommensurable. This seems to imply that there is no way of comparing or rationally adjudicating the claims of these values *wherever* they conflict. But no one could believe this, since obviously there are possible changes by which (say) such a trivial gain in equality was bought by such an enormous sacrifice of liberty that no one who believed in liberty at all could rationally favour it. So either it is false that these values are, as such, incommensurable, or incommensurability is a less discouraging or, again, deep feature than had been supposed.

Despite these objections, the claim that values are incommensurable does say something true and important. In fact, it says more than one true and important thing. There are at least four different denials which the claim can be taken to involve; they are of increasing strength, so that accepting one later in the list involves accepting those earlier.

1. There is no one currency in terms of which each conflict of values can be resolved.

2. It is not true that for each conflict of values, there is some value, independent of any of the conficting values, which can be appealed to in order to resolve that conflict.

3. It is not true that for each conflict of values, there is some value which can be appealed to (independent or not) in order rationally to resolve that conflict.

4. No conflict of values can ever rationally be resolved.
(4) is the position which the objector elicited from incommensurability, and which he rightly claimed to be too despairing. But that leaves the others, and these are not trivial or shallow positions.

Among these, (1) raises an interesting question, which goes beyond that particular proposition. Obviously incommensurability must in some way involve (1). Yet at the same time, there is a sense in which someone claiming the incommensurability of values could even accept that (1) was false, and admit that a universal currency of comparison was available, without this destroying the spirit of his claim, and this shows that the relations between that claim and the issue of rational choice between values is not as straightforward as it may seem. I shall assume that the only plausible candidate for such a universal currency of comparison would be utility (in some contemporary sense of people satisfying their preferences). The most basic version of the idea that utility provides a universal currency is that all values are versions or applications in some way of utility, and in this sense the claim that values are incommensurable of course rejects the idea of a universal currency. Indeed, in this version, it is not clear that there is really more than one value at all, or, consequently, real conflicts between values. Some indirect forms of utilitarianism, on the other hand, will want it to be the case both that there is a universal currency of utility and at the same time that the various values indirectly validated by reference to utility are autonomous enough for there to be recognisable conflicts between them. It is not clear how stable or coherent views of this kind are; in any case, they are equally rejected by the claim under discussion.

Both these versions of utilitarianism have the following feature: utility is the universal currency because the appeal to it is rationally *all of a piece* with the appeal to the other values. In the strongest version, utility is, so to speak, homogeneous with the other values – they are just versions of it. In the indirect version, the appeal to it is the application to a particular case of what is their justification in general. But someone who was not a utilitarian of either sort might think that utility indeed was the only possible universal resolver of conflicts, without however thinking that it was in this way homogeneous with other, conflicting, values at all. He could think that utility was another value, very different from and in certain respects perhaps even alien to other values, but that it did uniquely provide a last appeal from any conflict. I doubt that such a person could plausibly hold that utility was the only item which could ever be appealed to in resolving conflict. He is likely to think that some other values sometimes resolve some conflicts, but he might well think that utility was the only item that could always be appealed to when other appeals failed. He would have to be unduly optimistic, probably, about the sense that can be made of 'utility' itself, but – and this is the present point – he would not necessarily be going against the incommensurability claim. Although he thought that utility could be brought in as an arbiter to situations of conflict, he would see it as too outside the other values for that fact to count as a way of measuring them. This outlook would be a wider application of one we encountered in connection with the 'tragic' conflicts of obligations, where it was suggested that there might in a particular case indeed be something which it was better, all things considered, to do, and hence there were reasons for resolving the conflict in one way rather than the other, but that nevertheless that fact did not adequately meet the claims involved in the conflict.

(2), in so far as it is distinct from (1), seems obviously true, since unless there is a universal currency, it must surely be contingent whether there is some third value which can relevantly be brought in to decide some particular conflict. Moreover, there is a consideration similar to the one just discussed: if the deciding value were not intimately related to those involved in the conflict, we would have a decision, and a reason for it, but not one that supported any genuine commensurability of the values originally involved.

What about (3)? Here it might be wondered what processes were in question at all. How can one rationally resolve a conflict between two values by appealing to one of them? There is certainly one familiar pattern of argument which falls under this heading – that in which a conflict between values A and B is resolved, or at least alleviated, by the consideration that affirming A, though it may diminish B in some direction, will also lead to an increase of B in another. Thus proposals to increase equality, though at some cost of some people's liberty, are often defended with the consideration that they also increase some people's (not usually the same people's) liberty. Berlin himself has been very resistant to the reductionist aspects of this sort of argument, insisting that equality is one value and liberty is another. It is indeed true that they are two values, and neither can be reduced to the other; nevertheless, it is also true that increasing equality can increase liberty, and that can be one reason (besides the value of equality as a form of justice) for wanting to increase equality.

This kind of argument can, in my view, be sound, but it is not of course a type of argument which notably regards values as incommensurable. Its effect is precisely to bring the values A and B *in the particular case* nearer to commensurability. The holder of the incommensurability claim, resistant as he is to reduction of one value to another, will deny that this kind of argument is necessarily or even generally available, and will thus agree with (3). However, he need not be barred, it seems to me, from coming to a sort of conclusion referred to before, to the effect that in a given conflict between A and B, the amount gained in terms of A is (say) greater than the amount lost in terms of B. This might seem like a clear admission that A and B were commensurable; but this point seems to have force, I think, only because it is assumed that if A and B have these kinds of relations to one another in a given case, this must be because there is some one thing, more of which is gained along with A, in that case, than is lost along with B. But there need be no such thing, for this kind of conclusion to be sound, and if the supporter of the incommensurability claim is right, there will not in general by any such thing.

He will support all of (1), (2) and (3), and will be impressed also by the fact that sane and honourable people can attach different importance to different values, so that they will not agree on the resolution of many difficult conflict cases. However, it is important also in describing his position to include that resistance to Utopianism which I mentioned earlier. A Utopian theorist – let us consider one who uses the notion of *ideology* – might well agree with the account *of present society* in terms of irresoluble conflict, incommensurable values and so forth, and he would be resolutely opposed to analytical philosophers and others who seek to resolve those conflicts and reduce uncertainty by systematising our morality into an ethical theory – this itself must be an ideologically polluted enterprise. However, he will think that what needs to be transcended is present society, and that in some better condition conflict will be reduced, and false values discarded. Nor does he think that this will be a purely technological achievement, as we might all agree that conflict could be reduced and less refractory values established by drugs or brain-treatments; he sees it in terms of enlightenment or insight, though grounded, no doubt, in social action. The sceptic about Utopia doubts that there is anywhere for that kind of enlightenment or insight to come from, since his understanding of values as they are gives no hope that their present incoherences could be radically transcended without loss. You might perhaps bring about a society whose values were less conflicting, more clearly articulated, more efficient, and people, once arrived in this state, might have no sense of loss. But that would not mean there was no loss. It would mean that there was another loss, the loss of the sense of loss.

A Utopian theorist of ideology, and a pluralist sceptic about Utopia, can however agree on at least one thing, that the enterprise of trying to reduce our conflicts, and to legislate to remove moral uncertainty, by constructing a philosophical *ethical theory* (in the sense of systematising moral belief) is a misguided one. The ethical theorist tends to assimilate conflicts in moral belief to theoretical contradiction, and applies to moral understanding a model of theoretical rationality and adequacy. This is wrong in more than one way. If conflict among our values is not necessarily pathological, and if even where the situation is at fault, as with some conflicts of obligation, conflict is not a logical affliction of our thought, it must be a mistake to regard a need to eliminate conflict as a purely rational demand, of the kind that applies to a theoretical system. Rather we should see such needs as there are to reduce conflict and to rationalise our moral thought as having a more social and personal basis.

In particular, in a modern complex society functions which are ethically significant are performed by public agencies and, if the society is relatively open, this requires that they be governed by an explicable order which allows those agencies to be answerable. In a public, large and impersonal forum 'intuition' will not serve, though it will serve (and nothing else could serve) in personal life and in a more closely shared existence. This is well illustrated in connection with 'imperfect rationalisation', the situation in which some distinction, not further reasoned, can ground agreement in private and less impersonal connections, but may not serve, or may not continue to serve, where a public order demands a public answer. To take an example which has been recently discussed, a distinction between abortion, which is permitted, and infanticide, which is not, is one which can probably be naturally sustained in a certain context of shared moral sentiment without further reason being needed. The fact that further reason is not needed does not mean that that distinction is *irrational*. It means only that the basic distinction is more directly convincing than any reason that might be advanced for it: another way of putting it is that 'You can't kill that, it's a child' is more convincing as a reason than any reason which might be advanced for its being a reason. It may possibly be that in an open system (that is to say, in a system where explanations have to be given), where abortions are carried out by public and answerable agencies, such a context of moral sentiment can still survive, and be enough. But it may not, and a further requirement of rationalisation will be felt. If it is, then that requirement will not be a demand of pure rationality, but rather of a certain kind of public order. What this illustates in the area of 'imperfect rationalisation' applies also to the closely analogous cases of conflict.

These demands of the public order, however, have implications for private sentiment as well. There are also important needs, both of the individual and of the society, that private sentiment and the rules of the public order should not drift too far from each other. If functions which have specific moral significance (medical functions, for instance) are performed in an impersonal public sphere, and more activities which express and encourage important values are publicly conducted, some new accord must be found between private understanding, which can live with a good deal of 'intuition' and unresolved conflict, and the public order, which, unless we are to give up the ethical ambition that it be answerable, can only live with less. At the same time, the public order, if it is to carry conviction, and also not to flatten human experience, has to find ways in which it can be adequately related to private sentiment, which remains more 'intuitive' and open to conflict than public rules can be. For the intuitive condition is not only a state which private understanding *can* live with, but a state which it must have as part of its life, if that life is going to have any density or conviction and succeed in being that worthwhile kind of life which human beings lack unless they feel more than they can say, and grasp more than they can explain.

Rawls has written of a 'reflective equilibrium' between intuition (in the sense of moral conviction) and ethical theory, which it is the aim of moral philosophy to achieve. Rather, if philosophy is to understand the relations between conflict and rationalisation in the modern world, it should look towards an equilibrium – one to be achieved in practice – between private and public.

6 Justice as a virtue

I shall be particularly concerned with some points in Aristotle's treatment of justice in Book V of the *Nicomachean Ethics*, but the purpose is to raise some general questions about justice as a virtue of character. I am concerned with what Aristotle calls 'particular' justice, that is to say, with justice considered as one virtue of character among others. This disposition, he says, has two basic fields of application, the distributive and the rectificatory; this distinction will not concern us, and almost all the discussion can be referred to the first of this pair. Particular justice and injustice are concerned with a certain class of goods – 'those which are the subjects of good and bad luck, and which considered in themselves are always good, but not always good for a particular person' (1129b3–5). These are listed at 1130b3 as honour, money and safety: these are 'divisible' goods, which are such that if one person gets more, another characteristically gets less.

From the beginning, Aristotle associates particular injustice (*adikia*) with what he calls *pleonexia* – variously, greed, the desire to have more, the desire to have more than others. This characteristic Aristotle treats as the defining motive of particular injustice:

If one man commits adultery for the sake of gain, and makes money by it, while another does so from appetite, but loses money and is penalised for it, the latter would be thought self-indulgent rather than *pleonektēs*, while the former is unjust and not self-indulgent: this is obviously because of the fact that he gains. Again, all other unjust acts are ascribed in each case to some kind of vice, e.g. adultery to self-indulgence; deserting a fellow soldier, to cowardice; assaulting someone, to anger. But if he makes a gain, it is ascribed to no other vice but injustice. (1130a24 seq.).

This passage occurs in chapter 2, where Aristotle is concerned to find the distinguishing mark of particular injustice. It seems clear that the reference to 'unjust' acts is to acts which are unjust in the general sense – that is to say, roughly, wrong. Aristotle's point is that the way to pick out acts which are unjust in the particular sense from the whole range of acts which are contrary to justice in the general sense is by reference to the motive of *pleonexia* (which, on any showing, is excessively restricted, at this point of the discussion, to the desire for monetary gain). This is what the passage means; but its exact conclusion is unclear, and discussions of it do not pay enough attention to the Aristotelian distinction between unjust acts and an unjust character. It is one question, whether particular injustice as a vice is characterised by the motive of *pleonexia*; it is another question whether all acts which are unjust in the particular sense are motivated in that way. The two questions come together only if some quite complex assumptions are made, which I shall try to bring out.

Later in the book, Aristotle directly addresses the distinction between acts and character, and also applies his usual distinctions about responsibility. In chapter 8, he first considers acts done from ignorance, and makes various distinctions among these: of a person acting in this way involuntarily, he says that they act neither justly or unjustly except incidentally – they do things that merely happen to be just or unjust. Beyond this, if someone acts, not out of ignorance, but also not from deliberation, and, rather, from some passion, the act will indeed be an unjust act, but the agent will not be an unjust person. One who acts unjustly from deliberation is a person who possesses in the full sense the vice of injustice, and is fully an unjust person.

This, so far, is standard Aristotelian doctrine about bad acts and their relation to character and intention. Leaving aside acts which are involuntary through ignorance (more simply, unintentional), we can concentrate on the distinction, among intentional acts, between those which are the product of passion and later regretted, and those which are the expression of a settled disposition or vice of character. Considering acts which are, in the relevant aspect, intentional, and taking some undesirable characteristic V, it is the distinction between:

(A) those which are V acts but which are not the acts of a V person and

(B) those which are both V and the acts of a V person. The usual situation with the vices of character, in Aristotle's treatment, is that it will be a necessary condition of an act's being V that it is the product of some particular motive – lust, fear or whatever.

To be put alongside this is another distinction among acts, in terms of their motives: the distinction between those that are motivated by a desire for gain (*pleonexia*), and those that are motivated otherwise. Now the distinction between (A) and (B) standardly consists in this, that (A) acts are the episodic and later regretted expressions of a motive which regularly motivates the person who does (B) acts, that is to say, the person who is *V*. But it is obvious that an (A) unjust act need not be motivated by desire for gain at all. To take Aristotle's paradigmatic distribution case, a person could, on a particular occasion, be overcome by hopes of sexual conquest, or malice against one recipient, and so knowingly make an unjust distribution, and his act would surely be an unjust act.

Another of Aristotle's claims, admittedly an obscure one, indeed leads to this conclusion. In his rather unhappy and perfunctory account of the application of the mean to justice, he says: 'just action is intermediate between acting unjustly and being unjustly treated; for the one is to have too much and the other to have too little. Justice is a kind of mean, but not in the same way as the other virtues, but because it relates to an intermediate amount, while injustice relates to the extremes' (1133b3 seq.). It is not worth pursuing all the difficulties raised by these remarks, but one thing that the passage seems awkwardly to acknowledge is that, if *X* has been unjustly treated, then someone else (1138a15), *Y*, has acted unjustly towards him. But it cannot be a necessary condition of *X*'s being unjustly treated by *Y* that *Y* be motivated by the desire for gain, rather than by lust, malice, anger or whatever.

However, Aristotle is tempted by his standard model, according to which, since *pleonexia* is the motive of the unjust person, (A) acts of injustice must be episodic expressions of *pleonexia*. This idea issues in a desperate device at 1137a1 seq.: 'If [the distributor] judged unjustly with knowledge, he himself gets an unfair share of gratitude or revenge. As much, then, as if he had shared in the plunder, one who judges unjustly for these reasons gets too much.' There must be something wrong in extending *pleonexia* to cover someone's getting more of this kind of thing. What would it be in such a case to get the right amount of gratitude or revenge?

Aristotle correctly holds:

(a) one who knowingly produces an unjust distribution acts unjustly.

He also explicitly claims:

(b) the characteristic motive of the vice of injustice is the desire for gain.

In addition, he seems disposed to accept the standard model from which it will follow that:

(c) the difference between (A) acts and (B) acts of injustice is not of motive, but only a difference in the dispositional grounding of that motive.

The consequence of accepting all these claims is obviously false. There are acts which are unjust, and in the 'particular' sense, but which are the products of fear, jealousy, desire for revenge, etc. Moreover, they may be not merely episodic expressions of such motives. The cowardly man who runs away in battle acts not only in a cowardly way, but also unfairly, and does so because of his cowardice. Unjust acts which are not expressions of the vice of injustice can thus stem from other vices. But the motives characteristic of those other vices are not the motive of *pleonexia* supposedly characteristic of the vice of injustice. So we cannot, granted these truths, accept both (b) and (c).

It might be said that the cowardly man's act of injustice is in fact motivated by *pleonexia*, the desire for gain, as well as by fear: he is aiming at an unfair share of the divisible good of safety. That description, unlike the nonsense about an unfair share of gratitude or revenge, could contain some truth. But it will not do in order to straighten out Aristotle's account of the matter, since 1130a17 seq. makes it clear that *pleonexia* is seen as *contrasted* with such motives as fear, and not as coexisting with, or being a product of, such motives. The broader question of what *pleonexia* exactly is I shall come back to at the end.

(c) is one of the assumptions that I referred to earlier as needed to bring together the two questions, whether the unjust character is characterised by the motive of *pleonexia*, and whether all unjust acts are the product of that motive. (c) states that each unjust act must have the same motive as the unjust acts which are the product of an unjust character. That is surely wrong. We can recognise that it is wrong, however, only because we can identify certain intentional acts as unjust in the particular sense, and can do this without referring to their motive. Indeed we are helped by Aristotle in doing this, by his drawing our attention to such basic cases as the intentional misdistribution of divisible goods. Aristotle himself gives us a clear indication of the areas in which some unjust acts are to be found; in doing so, he also puts us in a strong position to deny, as he does not seem clearly to have done, the assumption (c).

However, the fact that some unjust acts can be located without referring to their motive does not entail that they all can be. It might be that some other unjust acts could be identified simply from their motive; in particular, by their flowing from a settled dispositional motive characteristic of the unjust character. In this case, they would not all have to be of the same types as those unjust acts which are identified independently of motive, such as misdistributions of divisible goods. They might, for instance, be acts of a sexual kind which, if motivated in a more usual way, would not be identified as having anything to do with particular injustice at all. Aristotle clearly thinks that there are acts of this kind. He associates the vice of *adikia* so closely with a certain motive (or rather, I shall suggest later, a certain class of motives), *pleonexia*, that he calls a person who is dispositionally motivated by that an *adikos*, and holds, in chapter 2, that any act which that person does from that motive is an act of particular injustice. Aristotle could of course go further, and hold that any act, of any kind, which is even episodically motivated by *pleonexia* is an unjust act in the particular sense. He would then have completed the equation of *adikia* and *pleonexia*, not only with respect to character, but with respect to acts. However, it is not clear to me that he does hold that: chapter 2, at any rate, seems to commit him only to the view that any act of a dispositionally pleonektic man which is an expression of his *pleonexia* is an unjust act.

I now turn to some questions about justice and injustice as states of character, independently, to some degree, of Aristotle's treatment. I shall concentrate on the area where our concepts most clearly overlap with Aristotle's, that of distributive justice. As a way of dealing with justice as a virtue, this concentration is obviously very selective, but the general shape of the conclusions will, I believe, apply more widely. In discussing distributive justice, I will not always assume, as Aristotle does, that we are concerned with some unallocated good which is, so to speak, 'up for grabs' and waiting to be distributed by some method or other to some class of recipients. We can, besides that, recognise also the case in which the good is already in somebody's hands, and the question is rather whether he justly holds it. We can extend the term 'distribution' to cover such possibilities.[1]

In the distributive case, we can distinguish three items to which the terms 'just' and 'unjust' can be applied: a distributor (if there is one), a method, and an outcome. The question basically raised by Aristotle's

---

[1] Nozick, who strongly emphasises this point in his *Anarchy, State and Utopia* (New York, 1974) calls the chapter in which this is discussed 'Distributive Justice'.

treatment concerns the relation between the first of these and the other two; but it is worth saying something about the relations between method and outcome, on the question of which, with respect to justice, has priority. Is a just outcome to be understood as one reached by a just method, or is a just method, more fundamentally, one that leads to just outcomes? At a first glance there seem to be examples which tell either way. Aristotle's own preferred examples tend to be ones in which the relevant merit or desert of the recipients is understood (at least by the distributor) beforehand, so that the basic idea is of a just outcome, namely that in which each recipient benefits in proportion to his desert, and a just method will be, derivatively, a method which brings about that outcome. On the other hand, it seems different if one takes a case in which some indivisible good has to be allocated among persons who have equal claims to it, and they agree to draw lots (a method which can be adapted also to cases in which they have unequal claims to it). Here the justice is not worn in its own right by the outcome of, say, Robinson's getting it, nor is it the fact that it has that outcome that makes the method just; it is rather the other way round.

This distinction is more fragile than it first looks, and is sensitive to the ways in which the outcome and the method are described. Thus if the method is itself described as that of allocating say, the food to the hungry, the 'desert' can come to characterise the method itself, and not merely the outcome. Not all the difficulties here are very interesting: they flow from an evident indeterminacy in the notions of method and outcome. But, even allowing for the difficulties, there is a class of cases in which the justice very specially rests in the method rather than in the particular outcome. In these, when we ask 'what makes it fair that *A* has it (*or* has that amount of it)?', the answer refers to a process by which *A* came to have the good in question, and, moreover, no characteristic of *A* which does not relate to that process is appropriately cited as grounding his claim to the good. This is true of Nozick's 'entitlement theory',[2] under which someone justly holds an item if he received it by an appropriate process (e.g. buying it) from someone who justly held it. Under such a theory, the process by which someone receives something is constitutive of the justice of his holding, and there is no independent assessment of the justice of the outcome at all.

[2] Op. cit. chapter 7.

This bears a resemblance, illuminating and also politically relevant, to another kind of case which also satisfies the condition for primacy of method, the case of allocation by lot. If Robinson draws the long straw, then what makes it fair that he gets the good is simply the fact that it was he who drew the straw. We may of course want to go further than that, and add that the straw-drawing was itself a method which, for instance, was agreed upon in advance. The fact that we can do this does not mean that the justice of the method ceases to be primary over the justice of the particular outcome: in explaining the fairness of Robinson's getting the good, we still essentially refer to the method. However, the point that we can, in the case of lots and similar processes, relevantly go on to say such things as that the method was agreed in advance, serves to bring out an important contrast with entitlement theory. In the case of lots, it is possible to ask questions about what makes the method a just or fair method.

The answer to those questions may even refer, in a general way, to outcomes. They will not refer to the particular outcome, and relative to that, the method remains primary, but some general relation of the method to outcomes may be relevant. For instance, a familiar argument in favour of a particular method of allocating some indivisible good would be that the probability it assigned to any given person of receiving the good was the same ratio as the share which that person, under the same general criteria, would appropriately receive of a divisible good (he gets one fifth of the cake, and a one in five chance of getting the chess set). A similar point emerges from the fact that lot-drawing can be modified, in certain circumstances, to allow for repeated trials; for instance, earlier winners may be excluded from later draws because it is thought fairer to increase over time the chances of a given person's winning. In such ways it is possible to criticise the fairness of methods such as drawing lots, by reference to general patterns of outcome, and by applying a notion of justice to such general patterns. But this resource seems mysteriously not available with Nozick's entitlement theory, and no other considerations, it seems, can be brought to bear on the question whether established methods of transfer are fair methods. But if we are to be convinced that the favoured transactions are not only just, but are unquestionably just, some special argument needs to be produced. It certainly does not simply follow from the truth that, relative to the particular case, the concept of 'justice' applies primarily to the method and derivatively to the outcome. That is a feature which Nozick's preferred methods of transfer share with other methods of distribution, where criticism of the methods is nevertheless possible.

For our present purposes, however, the priorities of method and outcome are a secondary issue. The main question concerns the relations of either of these to the notion of a just person, and from now on I shall speak of a 'just distribution' to cover both those cases in which the method would naturally be considered primary, and those in which it is more natural to pick on the outcome. The notion of a fair distribution is prior to that of a fair or just person. Such a person is one who is disposed to promote, look for, stand by, etc., just distributions, because that is what they are. He may also be good at inventing just distributions, by thinking of a good method or proposing an acceptable distribution in a particular case (this will be a characteristic of Aristotle's *epieikēs* (1137b 34), the person who is good at particular discriminations of fairness). But even there, it is important that, although it took him, or someone like him, to think of it, the distribution can then be recognised as fair independently of that person's character. It cannot rest on his previous record that some particular distribution, which perhaps seems entirely whimsical, is just (except in the sense, uninteresting to the present question, that his past record may encourage us to believe that there are other considerations involved in the present case, known to him though invisible to us).

The disposition of justice will lead the just person to resist unjust distributions – and to resist them *however they are motivated*. This applies, very centrally, to himself. There are many enemies to fair conduct, both episodic and dispositional, and the person of just character is good at resisting them. This means that he will need, as Aristotle himself insists, other virtues as well: courage, for instance, and self-control. But the disposition of justice can itself provide a motive. The disposition to pursue justice and to resist injustice has its own special motivating thoughts. It is both necessary and sufficient to being a just person that one dispositionally promotes some courses as being just, and resists others as being unjust.

What then is the disposition of injustice? What is to be a dispositionally unjust or unfair person? The answer surely can only be that it is to lack the disposition of justice – at the limit, not to be affected or moved by considerations of fairness to all. It involves a tendency to act from some motives on which the just person will not act, and indeed to have some motives which the just person will not have at all. Important among the motives to injustice (though they seem rarely to be mentioned) are such things as laziness or frivolity. Someone can make an unfair decision because it is too much trouble, or too boring, to think about what would be fair. Differently, he may find the outcome funny or diverting. At the end of that line is someone who finds the outcome amusing or otherwise attractive just because it is unfair.

It is important that this last condition is not the central or most basic condition of being an unjust person. The thoughts that motivate the unjust do not characteristically use, in this upside-down way, the concepts of justice and injustice. Those concepts, however, do essentially figure in the thought of the just person. It is not untypical of the virtues that the virtuous person should be partly characterised by the way in which he thinks about situations, and by the concepts he uses. What is unusual about justice is that the just person is characterised by applying to outcomes and methods, in an analogous sense, the concept under which he himself falls; this is itself connected with the priority of the justice of distributions over justice of character.

On this account, there is no one motive characteristic of the unjust person, just as there is no one enemy of just distributions. In particular, the unjust person is not necesssarily greedy or anxious to get more for himself, and insofar as Aristotle connects injustice essentially with *pleonexia* he is mistaken.[3] The mistake can, moreover, be fairly easily diagnosed at the systematic level: the vice of injustice has been over-assimilated to the other vices of character, so that Aristotle seeks a characteristic motive to go with it, whereas it must be basic to this vice, unlike others, that it does not import a special motive, but rather the lack of one.

The point is not merely that 'injustice' is not the name of a motive. Beyond that, there is no particular motive which the unjust person, because of his injustice, necessarily displays. In particular, he does not necessarily display *pleonexia*, which, whatever else needs to be said about it, certainly involves the idea of wanting something for oneself.

[3] *Insofar as*: someone might, instead, want to draw the conclusion that 'injustice' is an imperfect translation of *adikia*. It is true that the Aristotelian structure of *dikaiosynē – adikia*, taken as a whole, by no means corresponds totally to our concepts of justice and injustice, but in the areas under discussion here, the fit is in other respects very good.

Not all the motives that operate against justice, and gain expression in the unjust person, fit this pattern – not even all the important ones do so.

Beyond this, however, what is *pleonexia*? Is it even a motive itself? To call someone *pleonektēs* surely does ascribe certain motives to him, but motives which are very indeterminately specified. The *pleonektēs* wants more, but there must be something in particular of which in a given case he wants more. But 'more' than what? More than is fair or just, certainly, but he does not characteristically want it in those terms – he has no special passion for affronting justice, and, like the unjust person generally, he is not specially interested in using the concepts of justice and injustice at all. It is rather that he wants more than he has got, or that he wants more than others. Now anyone who wants anything that admits of more or less wants more than he has got, or at least more than he thinks that he has got; but when this becomes a recursive condition, it is called greediness, and that is certainly one sense of *pleonexia*. Such a person does not necessarily, or even typically, worry about comparisons with others. But in another, and probably the most important, sense of '*pleonexia*', comparisons with others are the point, and the notion of having more than others is included in the motivating thought. The application to such goods as money, or honour, or the Nobel Prize, is obvious.

The case of Aristotle's third divisible good, safety, is more difficult. To want *more safety than others* is surely an odd want, if that is its most basic intentional description; what one wants is *as much safety as possible* – enough, one hopes, to keep one safe. Of course, since safety is in the circumstances a divisible good, the steps taken to satisfy this want will involve, and may be aimed at, taking away other people's safety (pushing them out of the fall-out shelter). Thus the actions involved are much the same as with cases of *pleonexia*, but there is still a significant difference. With the Achillean *pleonektēs* of honour, an essential part of his satisfaction is that others do not have what he has. The Thersitean *pleonektēs* of safety, on the other hand, does not mind how many are eventually saved, so long as he is, and, for this reason, his *pleonexia* is a different thing. The important point is that *pleonexia* is not, in his case, ultimately a motive at all. He is a coward, with a keen understanding that safety is a divisible good, and no sense of justice. Thus even in some cases of the egoistic desire for a divisible good, *pleonexia* is not the most basic or illuminating way of characterising what is wrong with the man who does not care about justice. The love of competitive honour, on the other hand, is essentially pleonektic, and straight-forwardly directed at making sure that others do not get it instead of oneself.

'*Pleonexia*' can cover both greed and competitiveness. It certainly refers to a class of motives, rather than any single motive. Those who are pleonektic of some things are not usually pleonektic of everything. As Aristotle well knew, those who are pleonektic of honour are not necessarily pleonektic of money, and, conversely, and if there is anyone who is pleonektic of safety, it is certainly not Achilles. These various motives have no doubt at all times fuelled some of the most settled indifference to justice, but it is a mistake, one which dogs Aristotle's account, to look for something other than that settled indifference itself to constitute the vice of injustice, and, having looked for it, to find it in such motives.

7   Rawls and Pascal's wager

Rawls' argument for his two principles of justice,[1] based as it is on an analogy to a rational decision under uncertainty, bears a notable resemblance to another argument designed to lead to momentous moral consequences under conditions of uncertainty, namely Pascal's famous Wager argument to the effect that, it being uncertain whether God exists or not, it must be a rational strategy to behave as if he did. I want to explore the resemblances between the two arguments. My conclusion will be that Rawls' argument shares some faults with Pascal's, but that in addition its premises are even less enticing than Pascal's. Comparing the two arguments encourages the conclusion, I think, that the decision-theoretic element in Rawls' theory is not convincing.

The argument is, famously, an enormous elaboration and sophistication of the intuitively very appealing idea that a system or set of rules will be a fair one with respect to certain parties if they could all agree on it in advance of knowing what special position in the system, or relation to the rules, they might turn out to have. The intent of the theory (or rather, of this initial part of it: much else happens in Rawls' theory besides) is, on the lines of this idea, to represent moral considerations used by real people under conditions of knowledge in the form of self-interested considerations which would appeal to hypothetical (and entirely notional) people choosing a social system and sets of rules under conditions of very extensive, but not total, ignorance. The situation in which these choices are to be made, behind the 'veil of ignorance', is called the Original Position. It has a considerable number of conditions attached to it. A lot of arguments

[1] John Rawls, *A Theory of Justice* (Oxford, 1972). My discussion relates mostly to very familiar features of the theory, and I have not thought it necessary to give continuous references. Chapter III contains almost all the relevant material, particularly in sections 24–9; but see also Chapter II, section 15, for the index of primary goods as the substitute for utilities in the evaluation of the outcomes of choices made in the Original Position.

can be raised about these conditions, but I do not want to pursue these beyond making three points which are particularly relevant here. They all concern respects in which Rawls' handling of the supposedly self-interested choice made by the contracting parties pushes it more in the direction of an *un*self-interested choice than the root idea would have led one to expect.

First, it is accepted as a constraint on the choice made that it should be *final*, and this is interpreted to mean that the parties will not have reasons, when the veil of ignorance is lifted, to go back on it. Rawls extracts quite a lot from this condition, and it is the respect, as he remarks, in which the specifically *contractual* aspect of his theory does most work. But the sense in which he takes it is one, it seems to me, which involves the model being used too literally, as though what kept the parties to the social rules, when the veil is lifted, is a recollection of what they promised in the original position. But this is fictional. What will keep the social system and its rules going is whatever keeps such things going – and the question of what that may be is something which the parties in the Original Position will know about in virtue of their knowledge of the general principles of the social sciences. It is a reasonable structural requirement on the contract model that the parties should have reason to expect their agreement to stick, but whether it will do so is a matter of the empirical conditions of social stability in the sort of society they choose, and should be considered in that light. What Rawls in fact tends to do is to interpret the condition of finality in terms of whether the eventual system is perceived by its members *to be just*, and this in turn as whether they have good reason so to perceive it. But this comes perilously close to a requirement on the original choice, that it be of a system which *will be just* – which of course would be to moralise the original choice itself, and to put in at the beginning what we are supposed to get out at the end.

The next matter concerns the measures that the contracting parties can, in prospect, apply to the various outcomes. Of course, since they do not know their own eventual position, they cannot apply any measures to their own position as such – the issue is, by what criteria the various outcomes can, from the point of view of various representative positions within them, be ranked. Rawls is anxious to make it clear that these measures cannot consist in utilities, and hence that the choice made in the Original Position cannot actually be regarded as a decision-theoretical choice, but only as an analogy to a decision-theoretical choice. I take it that he does not want to deny that the reasoning is like that of decision-theory (maximin, the guiding notion, is after all a decision-theoretic concept), but that the values in terms of which outcomes are evaluated are different. Leaving aside the point – which we shall come back to – that there are no probabilities available, the distinction comes out in this, that the parties cannot assess their own utilities, because behind the veil of ignorance they have no particularised conception of their own good. They have only an idea of the Primary Goods, which are things which anyone wants, because they are (more or less) the conditions of getting anything else. They include liberty and possessions. Thus the merits of various outcomes are represented to them in the Original Position in terms of a schedule of Primary Goods which roughly gives, in these terms, the value of various positions within various outcomes. It is represented in money terms (in, as Rawls pedantically remarks, hundreds of dollars).

There is nothing inherently wrong in falling back on Primary Goods at this point, and, granted the rules of the game, there is not much else that could be done. But it underlines the peculiarity of the game. Any actual concrete social outcome would include people who took different views of the ranking of the primary goods – indeed, it needs no very ambitiously deterministic theory to suppose that the view they took on that matter would itself be a characteristic of and a product of their society. Rawls' people can cash it all out in terms of Primary Goods even in the Original Position, and it is indeed built in right from the beginning that they have a preference for liberty over other goods. But this feature of the choice situation must bias the outcome. The preference for liberty is not of course intrinsically altruistic: it is a preference for one's own liberty (or more precisely, for the liberty of anyone one may turn out to be). But the strong preference for liberty is part of outlook in which men are in general seen as essentially autonomous beings, and Rawls is disposed to explicate it in terms of a Kantian view of human relations. This view is not supposed to be that of his contracting parties, but the choice they are pictured as making seems – to put it mildly – to make most sense when they are understood as already possessing this view themselves. To the extent that they have this view themselves, to that extent their views would seem to be already moralised.

Last, there is the central and much-discussed question of their attitude to risk. Rawls is emphatic that the principles chosen should not depend on special attitudes to risk – for one thing, the parties cannot know, under the veil of ignorance, what their own attitude to risk is.

Now in making this claim Rawls does not mean that nothing can be said about their eventual choice as to whether it is risky, rash, or conservative. It clearly is conservative, and, in taking the maximin choice (which optimises the position of the least advantaged person) they make the safest choice available to them. Moreover, that this is so is one of their reasons for making it. When Rawls says that there is no special attitude to risk involved, he must mean that this is not a case in which there is a range of solutions, each rational in terms of a different attitude to risk: here, there is just one rational solution. His reasons for thinking this depend on two sorts of factors, the structure of the problem, and the parties' responsibilities. My immediate point concerns the second. A particular reason why the parties should take the safe choice is, Rawls says, the burden of commitment they bear with regard to later generations – they are operating as though they were responsible for a trust. But this surely represents once more an excessively altruistic extension of their concerns. The contracting parties were indeed introduced as fathers of families, with a natural concern for one generation ahead, but the way in which Rawls speaks of their commitment to not taking risks implies a heavier, and surely already moralised, onus of responsibility towards posterity. Once again, the argument is helped by the contracting parties being more than self-interested.

Besides responsibilities to future generations, there are features of the choice-situation itself which supposedly force the maximin solution. Rawls summarises them as these: there are no probabilities available – the parties have just no idea what chance they have of ending up in what position in e.g. a slave-owning society; they have no great interest in benefits over the minimum; and the worst of the bad alternatives involve 'grave risks', which 'one could hardly accept' (p. 154). (The second, and apparently very substantial, assumption ties up with their strong preference for liberty which I have already mentioned, and which I shall come back to.) The last of these propositions comes to saying that the worst one might get by taking a non-Rawlsian choice is very much worse than the worst one would get by taking a Rawlsian choice; in an obvious representation,

$(R1)$ $\overline{R}$ (min) is very much worse than R (min).

The second proposition, that they have no great interest in benefits over the minimum, can be simplified for the present purpose into the statement that benefits over the minimum are not regarded by them as so great benefits, as are benefits up to the minimum – this means we can leave out the distinction which Rawls imports, between what they regard as benefits, and the interest they take in those benefits. This second proposition can then be put as:

(R2) $\bar{R}$ (max) is not very much better than R (min).

We now come to Pascal's Wager.[2] Pascal's argument depended on certain assumptions. One was that there were two relevant alternatives: that the Christian God did not exist, or that he did exist, and that he sent believers to Heaven, and unbelievers to Hell. Next, Pascal assumed that there were certain actions which could lead to belief: if you started by insincerely acting as though God existed, you would end up sincerely acting so, i.e. believing in God. The Wager argument was designed to show the waverer the rationality of so acting. He cannot be certain that God does not exist. But the disadvantage of being an unbeliever if the worst happens and God turns out to exist (i.e. going to Hell) is evidently vastly greater than the worst that can happen if one is a believer – namely, that God should not exist and one should have wasted one's time in going to church, passing over some pleasures etc. Or, as we may put it

(P1) $\bar{B}$ (min) is very much worse than B (min).

On the other hand, the best you get as an unbeliever (pleasures, no church, etc., and no Hell), is not all that much better than the worst outcome for a believer (church, fewer pleasures, and no Heaven or Hell). That is,

(P2) $\bar{B}$ (max) is not very much better than B (min).

Thus, Pascal argued, it is rational to take the belief strategy in this highly uncertain situation. The argument is structurally the same as Rawls'. Now the premises of Pascal's argument are highly dubious. In particular, the partition of the possibilities is quite gratuitous. We could equally divide them up into there being or not being some other sort of God, who, if he existed, might not particularly favour Christians – as Diderot put it, 'An Imam could reason just as well this way.' Again, even if there is a Christian God, how do we know that his rewards follow in this way? He might, for instance, not much favour those who came to believe in him by such strategies.

Rawls' argument has its own parallel to this latter failing: one which in effect has already come up earlier, particularly in the discussion of finality. The objection in Pascal's case is that he has no reason to think that the outcomes of the courses of action are independent of the

---

[2] For a full account, see Ian Hacking, 'The Logic of Pascal's Wager', *American Philosophical Quarterly*, April, 1972, to which I am indebted.

strategic deliberation itself. It should be so in Rawls' case as well. What preferences people have in a social situation certainly depends in some part on what that social system is (a fact which will be known to the parties even behind the veil of ignorance, since it is a general truth), and what social system they will be in depends on the strategic choice. So Rawls' argument should be open to this point, but, as we have already seen, he in fact leaves this out by holding substantial assumptions about preference between Primary Goods constant over the different alternatives. This just weakens the force of the 'self-interested' model.

Pascal's argument, once one has got past the unacceptability of those premisses, is not too bad. This is because there is a special value attached to the inequality (P_1), since the badness of Hell is *infinite*, and by those standards (P_2) is certainly true, since any finite difference compared with that difference is vanishingly small. (This admittedly leaves out the consideration, hard to handle in this simple form of argument, that if God does not exist, then the difference between the items mentioned in (P_2) is the *biggest difference there is*). Moreover, the infinite awfulness of the worst outcome enables him to rely on the weakest possible probability premiss, that the probability of God's existence is non–zero. Even minimal probability is enough, if the cost of overlooking that possibility would be infinite.

But there is no such rationale in connexion with (R_1) and (R_2). Here there is no appeal to the finite and infinite, and correspondingly no recourse to minimal probabilities. Without *some* presumptions about probabilities, (R_1) and (R_2) could not provide enough basis for action. Even if we granted that they were both true, there must surely be some probability measures of $\bar{R}$ outcomes as against R outcomes which would make an $\bar{R}$ choice rational, and Rawls must at least be assuming that these do not obtain.

Moreover, as we have already seen in effect, (R_2) must rest both on a rather saintly view of things on the part of the contracting parties, and a quite unreasonable belief that they would retain such a saintly view if they were top dogs in a $\bar{R}$ society. While Rawls may agree to (R_2), there seems no reason to think that Tutankhamen would, and without *some* information on the chances of being Tutankhamen, there is no reason for the self-interested contractor to buy the maximin solution. Pascal's argument, granted its failings (at least one of which is shared, in a way, by Rawls'), can get some leverage out of its use of *infinity*; Rawls' lacks this resource and the comparison helps to bring out how under-powered the supposed rational choice under ignorance is.

Rawls' theory tries, in effect, to link politics with morality, and morality (or at least the relevant parts of it) to a self-interested choice under uncertainty. He indeed links politics with a Kantian conception of morality, but the supposed choice under uncertainty seems in fact to have the morality already packed into it, and as an exercise in decision theory, or anything like it, compares unfavourably even with Pascal's celebratedly bad bet.

8 Internal and external reasons

Sentences of the forms 'A has a reason to ϕ' or 'There is a reason for A to ϕ' (where 'ϕ' stands in for some verb of action) seem on the face of it to have two different sorts of interpretation. On the first, the truth of the sentence implies, very roughly, that A has some motive which will be served or furthered by his ϕ-ing, and if this turns out not to be so the sentence is false: there is a condition relating to the agent's aims, and if this is not satisfied it is not true to say, on this interpretation, that he has a reason to ϕ. On the second interpretation, there is no such condition, and the reason-sentence will not be falsified by the absence of an appropriate motive. I shall call the first the 'internal', the second the 'external', interpretation. (Given two such interpretations, and the two forms of sentence quoted, it is reasonable to suppose that the first sentence more naturally collects the internal interpretation, and the second the external, but it would be wrong to suggest that either form of words admits only one of the interpretations.)

I shall also for convenience refer sometimes to 'internal reasons' and 'external reasons', as I do in the title, but this is to be taken only as a convenience. It is a matter for investigation whether there are two sorts of reasons for action, as opposed to two sorts of statements about people's reasons for action. Indeed, as we shall eventually see, even the interpretation in one of the cases is problematical.

I shall consider first the internal interpretation, and how far it can be taken. I shall then consider, more sceptically, what might be involved in an external interpretation. I shall end with some very brief remarks connecting all this with the issue of public goods and free-riders.

The simplest model for the internal interpretation would be this: A has a reason to ϕ iff A has some desire the satisfaction of which will be served by his ϕ-ing. Alternatively, we might say...some desire, the satisfaction of which A believes will be served by his ϕ-ing; this difference will concern us later. Such a model is sometimes ascribed to Hume, but since in fact Hume's own views are more complex than this, we might call it *the sub-Humean model*. The sub-Humean model is certainly too simple. My aim will be, by addition and revision, to work it up into something more adequate. In the course of trying to do this, I shall assemble four propositions which seem to me to be true of internal reason statements.

Basically, and by definition, any model for the internal interpretation must display a relativity of the reason statement to the agent's *subjective motivational set*, which I shall call the agent's *S*. The contents of *S* we shall come to, but we can say:

(i) An internal reason statement is falsified by the absence of some appropriate element from *S*.

The simplest sub-Humean model claims that any element in *S* gives rise to an internal reason. But there are grounds for denying this, not because of regrettable, imprudent, or deviant elements in *S* – they raise different sorts of issues – but because of elements in *S* based on false belief.

The agent believes that this stuff is gin, when it is in fact petrol. He wants a gin and tonic. Has he reason, or a reason, to mix this stuff with tonic and drink it? There are two ways here (as suggested already by the two alternatives for formulating the sub-Humean model). On the one hand, it is just very odd to say that he has a reason to drink this stuff, and natural to say that he has no reason to drink it, although he thinks that he has. On the other hand, if he does drink it, we not only have an explanation of his doing so (a reason why he did it), but we have such an explanation which is of the reason-for-action form. This explanatory dimension is very important, and we shall come back to it more than once. If there are reasons for action, it must be that people sometimes act for those reasons, and if they do, their reasons must figure in some correct explanation of their action (it does not follow that they must figure in all correct explanations of their action). The difference between false and true beliefs on the agent's part cannot alter the *form* of the explanation which will be appropriate to his action. This consideration might move us to ignore the intuition which we noticed before, and lead us just to legislate that in the case of the agent who wants gin, he has a reason to drink this stuff which is petrol.

I do not think, however, that we should do this. It looks in the wrong direction, by implying in effect that the internal reason conception is only concerned with explanation, and not at all with the agent's rationality, and this may help to motivate a search for other sorts of reason which are connected with his rationality. But the internal reasons conception is concerned with the agent's rationality. What we can correctly ascribe to him in a third-personal internal reason statement is also what he can ascribe to himself as a result of deliberation, as we shall see. So I think that we should rather say:

(ii) A member of S, D, will not give A a reason for ϕ-ing if either the existence of D is dependent on false belief, or A's belief in the relevance of ϕ-ing to the satisfaction of D is false.

(This double formulation can be illustrated from the gin/petrol case: D can be taken in the first way as the desire to drink what is in this bottle, and in the second way as the desire to drink gin.) It will, all the same, be true that if he does ϕ in these circumstances, there was not only a reason why he ϕ-ed, but also that that displays him as, relative to his false belief, acting rationally.

We can note the epistemic consequence:

(iii) (a) A may falsely believe an internal reason statement about himself, and (we can add)

(b) A may not know some true internal reason statement about himself.

(b) comes from two different sources. One is that A may be ignorant of some fact such that if he did know it he would, in virtue of some element in S, be disposed to ϕ: we can say that he has a reason to ϕ, though he does not know it. For it to be the case that he actually has such a reason, however, it seems that the relevance of the unknown fact to his actions has to be fairly close and immediate; otherwise one merely says that A would have a reason to ϕ if he knew the fact. I shall not pursue the question of the conditions for saying the one thing or the other, but it must be closely connected with the question of when the ignorance forms part of the explanation of what A actually does.

The second source of (iii) is that A may be ignorant of some element in S. But we should notice that an unknown element in S, D, will provide a reason for A to ϕ only if ϕ-ing is rationally related to D; that is to say, roughly, a project to ϕ could be the answer to a deliberative question formed in part by D. If D is unknown to A because it is in the unconscious, it may well not satisfy this condition, although of course it may provide the reason why he ϕ's, that is, may explain or help to explain his ϕ-ing. In such cases, the ϕ-ing may be related to D only symbolically.

I have already said that

(iv) internal reason statements can be discovered in deliberative reasoning.

It is worth remarking the point, already implicit, that an internal reason statement does not apply only to that action which is the uniquely preferred result of the deliberation. '*A* has reason to φ' does not mean 'the action which *A* has overall, all-in, reason to do is φ-ing'. He can have reason to do a lot of things which he has other and stronger reasons not to do.

The sub-Humean model supposes that φ-ing has to be related to some element in *S* as causal means to end (unless, perhaps, it is straightforwardly the carrying out of a desire which is itself that element in *S*). But this is only one case: indeed, the mere discovery that some course of action is the causal means to an end is not in itself a piece of practical reasoning.[1] A clear example of practical reasoning is that leading to the conclusion that one has reason to φ because φ-ing would be the most convenient, economical, pleasant etc. way of satisfying some element in *S*, and this of course is controlled by other elements in *S*, if not necessarily in a very clear or determinate way. But there are much wider possibilities for deliberation, such as: thinking how the satisfaction of elements in *S* can be combined, e.g. by time-ordering; where there is some irresoluble conflict among the elements of *S*, considering which one attaches most weight to (which, importantly, does not imply that there is some one commodity of which they provide varying amounts); or, again, finding constitutive solutions, such as deciding what would make for an entertaining evening, granted that one wants entertainment.

As a result of such processes an agent can come to see that he has reason to do something which he did not see he had reason to do at all. In this way, the deliberative process can add new actions for which there are internal reasons, just as it can also add new internal reasons for given actions. The deliberative process can also subtract elements from *S*. Reflection may lead the agent to see that some belief is false, and hence to realise that he has in fact no reason to do something he thought he had reason to do. More subtly, he may think he has reason to promote some development because he has not exercised his

---

[1] A point made by Aurel Kolnai: see his 'Deliberation is of Ends', in *Ethics, Value and Reality* (London and Indianapolis, 1978). See also David Wiggins, 'Deliberation and Practical Reason', *PAS*, LXXVI (1975–6); reprinted in part in *Practical Reasoning*, ed. J. Raz (Oxford, 1978).

imagination enough about what it would be like if it came about. In his unaided deliberative reason, or encouraged by the persuasions of others, he may come to have some more concrete sense of what would be involved, and lose his desire for it, just as, positively, the imagination can create new possibilities and new desires. (These are important possibilities for politics as well as for individual action.)

We should not, then, think of S as statically given. The processes of deliberation can have all sorts of effect on S, and this is a fact which a theory of internal reasons should be very happy to accommodate. So also it should be more liberal than some theorists have been about the possible elements in S. I have discussed S primarily in terms of desires, and this term can be used, formally, for all elements in S. But this terminology may make one forget that S can contain such things as dispositions of evaluation, patterns of emotional reaction, personal loyalties, and various projects, as they may be abstractly called, embodying commitments of the agent. Above all, there is of course no supposition that the desires or projects of an agent have to be egoistic; he will, one hopes, have non-egoistic projects of various kinds, and these equally can provide internal reasons for action.

There is a further question, however, about the contents of S: whether it should be taken, consistently with the general idea of internal reasons, as containing *needs*. It is certainly quite natural to say that A has a reason to pursue X, just on the ground that he needs X, but will this naturally follow in a theory of internal reasons? There is a special problem about this only if it is possible for the agent to be unmotivated to pursue what he needs. I shall not try to discuss here the nature of needs, but I take it that insofar as there are determinately recognisable needs, there can be an agent who lacks any interest in getting what he indeed needs. I take it, further, that that lack of interest can remain after deliberation, and, also that it would be wrong to say that such a lack of interest must always rest on false belief. (Insofar as it does rest on false belief, then we can accommodate it under (ii), in the way already discussed.)

If an agent really is uninterested in pursuing what he needs; and this is not the product of false belief; and he could not reach any such motive from motives he has by the kind of deliberative processes we have discussed; then I think we do have to say that in the internal sense he indeed has no reason to pursue these things. In saying this, however, we have to bear in mind how strong these assumptions are, and how seldom we are likely to think that we know them to be true. When we say that a person has reason to take medicine which he needs, although he consistently and persuasively denies any interest in preserving his health, we may well still be speaking in the internal sense, with the thought that really at some level he *must* want to be well.

However, if we become clear that we have no such thought, and persist in saying that the person has this reason, then we must be speaking in another sense, and this is the external sense. People do say things that ask to be taken in the external interpretation. In James' story of Owen Wingrave, from which Britten made an opera, Owen's family urge on him the necessity and importance of his joining the army, since all his male ancestors were soldiers, and family pride requires him to do the same. Owen Wingrave has no motivation to join the army at all, and all his desires lead in another direction: he hates everything about military life and what it means. His family might have expressed themselves by saying that *there was a reason for Owen to join the army.* Knowing that there was nothing in Owen's *S* which would lead, through deliberative reasoning, to his doing this would not make them withdraw the claim or admit that they made it under a misapprehension. They mean it in an external sense. What is that sense?

A preliminary point is that this is not the same question as that of the status of a supposed categorical imperative, in the Kantian sense of an 'ought' which applies to an agent independently of what the agent happens to want: or rather, it is not undoubtedly the same question. First, a categorical imperative has often been taken, as by Kant, to be necessarily an imperative of morality, but external reason statements do not necessarily relate to morality. Second, it remains an obscure issue what the relation is between 'there is a reason for *A* to...' and '*A* ought to...' Some philosophers take them to be equivalent, and under that view the question of external reasons of course comes much closer to the question of a categorical imperative. However, I shall not make any assumption about such an equivalence, and shall not further discuss 'ought'.[2]

In considering what an external reason statement might mean, we have to remember again the dimension of possible explanation, a consideration which applies to any reason for action. If something can be a reason for action, then it could be someone's reason for acting on a particular occasion, and it would then figure in an explanation of that action. Now no external reason statement could *by itself* offer an explanation of anyone's action. Even if it were true (whatever that

[2] It is discussed in chapter 9, below.

might turn out to mean) that there was a reason for Owen to join the army, that fact by itself would never explain anything that Owen did, not even his joining the army. For if it was true at all, it was true when Owen was not motivated to join the army. The whole point of external reason statements is that they can be true independently of the agent's motivations. But nothing can explain an agent's (intentional) actions except something that motivates him so to act. So something else is needed besides the truth of the external reason statement to explain action, some psychological link; and that psychological link would seem to be belief. *A*'s believing an external reason statement about himself may help to explain his action.

External reason statements have been introduced merely in the general form 'there is a reason for *A* to...', but we now need to go beyond that form, to specific statements of reasons. No doubt there are some cases of an agent's ϕ-ing because he believes that there is a reason for him to ϕ, while he does not have any belief about what that reason is. They would be cases of his relying on some authority whom he trusts, or, again, of his recalling that he did know of some reason for his ϕ-ing, but his not being able to remember what it was. In these respects, reasons for action are like reasons for belief. But, as with reasons for belief, they are evidently secondary cases. The basic case must be that in which *A* ϕ's, not because he believes only that there is some reason or other for him to ϕ, but because he believes of some determinate consideration that it constitutes a reason for him to ϕ. Thus Owen Wingrave might come to join the army because (now) he believes that it is a reason for him to do so that his family has a tradition of military honour.

Does believing that a particular consideration is a reason to act in a particular way provide, or indeed constitute, a motivation to act? If it does not, then we are no further on. Let us grant that it does – this claim indeed seems plausible, so long at least as the connexion between such beliefs and the disposition to act is not tightened to that unnecessary degree which excludes *akrasia*. The claim is in fact *so* plausible, that this agent, with this belief, appears to be one about whom, now, an *internal* reason statement could truly be made: he is one with an appropriate motivation in his *S*. A man who does believe that considerations of family honour constitute reasons for action is a man with a certain disposition to action, and also dispositions of approval, sentiment, emotional reaction, and so forth.

Now it does not follow from this that there is nothing in external reason statements. What does follow is that their content is not going to be revealed by considering merely the state of one who believes such a statement, nor how that state explains action, for that state is merely the state with regard to which an internal reason statement could truly be made. Rather, the content of the external type of statement will have to be revealed by considering what it is to *come to believe* such a statement – it is there, if at all, that their peculiarity will have to emerge.

We will take the case (we have implicitly been doing so already) in which an external reason statement is made about someone who, like Owen Wingrave, is not already motivated in the required way, and so is someone about whom an internal statement could not also be truly made. (Since the difference between external and internal statements turns on the implications accepted by the speaker, external statements can of course be made about agents who are already motivated; but that is not the interesting case.) The agent does not presently believe the external statement. If he comes to believe it, he will be motivated to act; so coming to believe it must, essentially, involve acquiring a new motivation. How can that be?

This is closely related to an old question, of how 'reason can give rise to a motivation', a question which has famously received from Hume a negative answer. But in that form, the question is itself unclear, and is unclearly related to the argument – for of course reason, that is to say, rational processes, can give rise to new motivations, as we have seen in the account of deliberation. Moreover, the traditional way of putting the issue also (I shall suggest) picks up an onus of proof about what is to count as a 'purely rational process' which not only should it not pick up, but which properly belongs with the critic who wants to oppose Hume's general conclusion and to make a lot out of external reason statements – someone I shall call 'the external reasons theorist'.

The basic point lies in recognising that the external reasons theorist must conceive *in a special way* the connexion between acquiring a motivation and coming to believe the reason statement. For of course there are various means by which the agent could come to have the motivation and also to believe the reason statement, but which are the wrong kind of means to interest the external reasons theorist. Owen might be so persuaded by his family's moving rhetoric that he acquired both the motivation and the belief. But this excludes an element which the external reasons theorist essentially wants, that the agent should acquire the motivation *because* he comes to believe the reason statement, and that he should do the latter, moreover, because, in some way, he is considering the matter aright. If the theorist is to hold on to these conditions, he will, I think, have to make the condition under which the agent appropriately comes to have the motivation something like this, that he should deliberate correctly; and the external reasons statement itself will have to be taken as roughly equivalent to, or at least as entailing, the claim that if the agent rationally deliberated, then, whatever motivations he originally had, he would come to be motivated to ϕ.

But if this is correct, there does indeed seem great force in Hume's basic point, and it is very plausible to suppose that all external reason statements are false. For, *ex hypothesi*, there is no motivation for the agent to deliberate *from*, to reach this new motivation. Given the agent's earlier existing motivations, and this new motivation, what has to hold for external reason statements to be true, on this line of interpretation, is that the new motivation could be in some way rationally arrived at, granted the earlier motivations. Yet at the same time it must not bear to the earlier motivations the kind of rational relation which we considered in the earlier discussion of deliberation – for in that case an internal reason statement would have been true in the first place. I see no reason to suppose that these conditions could possibly be met.

It might be said that the force of an external reason statement can be explained in the following way. Such a statement implies that a rational agent would be motivated to act appropriately, and it can carry this implication, because a rational agent is precisely one who has a general disposition in his *S* to do what (he believes) there is reason for him to do. So when he comes to believe that there is reason for him to ϕ, he is motivated to ϕ, even though, before, he neither had a motive to ϕ, nor any motive related to ϕ-ing in one of the ways considered in the account of deliberation.

But this reply merely puts off the problem. It reapplies the desire and belief model (roughly speaking) of explanation to the actions in question, but using a desire and a belief the content of which are in question. *What* is it that one comes to believe when he comes to believe that there is reason for him to ϕ, if it is not the proposition, or something that entails the proposition, that if he deliberated rationally, he would be motivated to act appropriately? We were asking how any true proposition could have that content; it cannot help, in answering that, to appeal to a supposed desire which is activated by a belief which has that very content.

These arguments about what it is to accept an external reason statement involve some idea of what is possible under the account of deliberation already given, and what is excluded by that account. But here it may be objected that the account of deliberation is very vague, and has for instance allowed the use of the imagination to extend or restrict the contents of the agent's S. But if that is so, then it is unclear what the limits are to what an agent might arrive at by rational deliberation from his existing S.

It *is* unclear, and I regard it as a basically desirable feature of a theory of practical reasoning that it should preserve and account for that unclarity. There is an essential indeterminacy in what can be counted a rational deliberative process. Practical reasoning is a heuristic process, and an imaginative one, and there are no fixed boundaries on the continuum from rational thought to inspiration and conversion. To someone who thinks that reasons for action are basically to be understood in terms of the internal reasons model, this is not a difficulty. There is indeed a vagueness about '*A* has reason to ϕ', in the internal sense, insofar as the deliberative processes which could lead from *A*'s present S to his being motivated to ϕ may be more or less ambitiously conceived. But this is no embarrassment to those who take as basic the internal conception of reasons for action. It merely shows that there is a wider range of states, and a less determinate one, than one might have supposed, which can be counted as *A*'s having a reason to ϕ.

It is the external reasons theorist who faces a problem at this point. There are of course many things that a speaker may say to one who is not disposed to ϕ when the speaker thinks that he should be, as that he is inconsiderate, or cruel, or selfish, or imprudent; or that things, and he, would be a lot nicer if he were so motivated. Any of these can be sensible things to say. But one who makes a great deal out of putting the criticism in the form of an external reason statement seems concerned to say that what is particularly wrong with the agent is that he is *irrational*. It is this theorist who particularly needs to make this charge precise: in particular, because he wants any rational agent, as such, to acknowledge the requirement to do the thing in question.

Owen Wingrave's family may not have expressed themselves in terms of 'reasons', but, as we imagined, they could have used the external reasons formulation. This fact itself provides some difficulty for the external reasons theorist. This theorist, who sees the truth of an external reason statement as potentially grounding a charge of irrationality against the agent who ignores it, might well want to say that if the Wingraves put their complaints against Owen in this form, they would very probably be claiming something which, in this particular case, was false. What the theorist would have a harder time showing would be that the words used by the Wingraves *meant* something different from what they mean when they are, as he supposes, truly uttered. But what they mean when uttered by the Wingraves is almost certainly *not* that rational deliberation would get Owen to be motivated to join the army – which is (very roughly) the meaning or implication we have found for them, if they are to bear the kind of weight such theorists wish to give them.

The sort of considerations offered here strongly suggest to me that external reason statements, when definitely isolated as such, are false, or incoherent, or really something else misleadingly expressed. It is in fact harder to isolate them in people's speech than the introduction of them at the beginning of this chapter suggested. Those who use these words often seem, rather, to be entertaining an optimistic internal reason claim, but sometimes the statement is indeed offered as standing definitely outside the agent's *S* and what he might derive from it in rational deliberation, and then there is, I suggest, a great unclarity about what is meant. Sometimes it is little more than that things would be better if the agent so acted. But the formulation in terms of reasons does have an effect, particularly in its suggestion that the agent is being irrational, and this suggestion, once the basis of an internal reason claim has been clearly laid aside, is bluff. If this is so, the only real claims about reasons for action will be internal claims.

A problem which has been thought to lie very close to the present subject is that of public goods and free riders, which concerns the situation (very roughly) in which each person has egoistic reason to want a certain good provided, but at the same time each has egoistic reason not to take part in providing it. I shall not attempt any discussion of this problem, but it may be helpful, simply in order to make clear my own view of reasons for action and to bring out contrasts with some other views, if I end by setting out a list of questions which bear on the problem, together with the answers that would be given to them by one who thinks (to put it cursorily) that the only rationality of action is the rationality of internal reasons.

1. Can we define notions of rationality which are not purely egoistic?

   Yes.

2. Can we define notions of rationality which are not purely means–end?

   Yes.

3. Can we define a notion of rationality where the action rational for *A* is in no way relative to *A*'s existing motivations?

   No.

4. Can we show that a person who only has egoistic motivations is irrational in not pursuing non-egoistic ends?

   Not necessarily, though we may be able to in special cases. (The trouble with the egoistic person is not characteristically irrationality.)

Let there be some good, *G*, and a set of persons, *P*, such that each member of *P* has egoistic reason to want *G* provided, but delivering *G* requires action *C*, which involves costs, by each of some proper sub-set of *P*; and let *A* be a member of *P*: then

5. Has *A* egoistic reason to do *C* if he is reasonably sure either that too few members of *P* will do *C* for *G* to be provided, or that enough other members of *P* will do *C*, so that *G* will be provided?

   No.

6. Are there any circumstances of this kind in which *A* can have egoistic reason to do *C*?

   Yes, in those cases in which reaching the critical number of those doing *C* is sensitive to his doing *C*, or he has reason to think this.

7. Are there any motivations which would make it rational for *A* to do *C*, even though not in the situation just referred to?

   Yes, if he is not purely egoistic: many. For instance, there are expressive motivations – appropriate e.g. in the celebrated voting case.[3] There are also motivations which derive from the

---

[3] A well-known treatment is by M. Olson Jr. *The Logic of Collective Action* (Cambridge, Mass., 1965). On expressive motivations in this connexion, see S. I. Benn, 'Rationality and Political Behaviour', in S. I. Benn and G. W. Mortimore, eds., *Rationality and the Social Sciences* (London, 1976). On the point about fairness, which follows in the

sense of fairness. This can precisely transcend the dilemma of 'either useless or unnecessary', by the form of argument 'somebody, but no reason to omit any particular body, so everybody'.

8. It is irrational for an agent to have such motivations?

   In any sense in which the question is intelligible, no.

9. Is it rational for society to bring people up with these sorts of motivations?

   Insofar as the question is intelligible, yes. And certainly we have reason to encourage people to have these dispositions – e.g. in virtue of possessing them ourselves.

I confess that I cannot see any other major questions which, at this level of generality, bear on these issues. All these questions have clear answers which are entirely compatible with a conception of practical rationality in terms of internal reasons for action, and are also, it seems to me, entirely reasonable answers.

---

text, there is of course a very great deal more to be said: for instance, about how members of a group can, compatibly with fairness, converge on strategies more efficient than everyone's doing C (such as people taking turns).

9   *Ought* and moral obligation

Many and various attempts have been made to distinguish different senses of the English term *ought*. Harman, for instance,[1] has written: 'A sentence like "Jones ought to take a vacation" intuitively has at least four different interpretations.' These are said to express: likelihood; desirability, in the sense of something 'being appropriate', as in 'there ought to be more love in the world'; what Harman calls 'a moral sense'; and 'a prudential sense'. The first of these certainly exists, even if it is a little strained as applied to the particular example, but it will not concern us further here; in this, as in many other respects, the present discussion makes no pretensions at all to giving a complete account of the term. The so-called 'prudential sense', again, we shall come back to later, although it is certainly not well picked out by that phrase. The first question I shall discuss concerns the second and third of the senses which Harman distinguishes. The way in which these two are labelled does not in fact reveal the main point at issue. Clearly the label 'a moral sense' cannot succeed in distinguishing anything totally from the second sense, since there is such a thing as moral desirability or appropriateness – indeed the very example of the desire for more love in the world is said to express a moral sentiment. If there is a notion to be isolated here, it seems to have something to do with a more restricted moral notion, such as that of obligation.

Harman claims to detect two kinds of *ought* sentence, distinguished by a difference of logical form. He supposes that a test for this lies in the appropriateness of the active/passive transform. Consider for instance the relations between

(1) Jones ought to have examined Smith

and

(2) Smith ought to have been examined by Jones.

[1] G. Harman, review of Wertheimer's *The Significance of Sense*, *Philosophical Review*, LXXXII (1973), pp. 235–9.

In some uses of *ought* (1) and (2) are equivalent; in others (1) may be appropriate but not (2). In particular, it is claimed that (2) will not be appropriate if (1) expresses an obligation of Jones'. Harman offers as a 'natural explanation' of this fact that 'there are at least two different uses of *ought* with different logical properties': in one it represents a property of a state of affairs, in another it represents a relation between an agent and a possible course of action. In the first case, one would expect equivalence under the active/passive transform (since two sentences related in this way presumably represent, if any two non-identical sentences do, the same state of affairs); in the second case one would not.

It is incontestable that there is a use of *ought* in which it does not express a property of an agent. It occurs, for example, in

(3) This room ought to be swept,

which can be represented as of the form '$O(p)$', with *ought* occurring as an operator on a proposition. This representation can be applied also to

(4) Somebody ought to sweep this room.

(4) is ambiguous, and it is clear that its ambiguity lies in a familiar ambiguity of scope. So there must at least be a derivative property of a person which *ought* can express, a property of the form: *being someone with regard to whom it ought to be the case that he...* This is a type of property that can be derived from any propositional operator which does not generate a completely opaque context, and *ought* is such a propositional operator.

However, it seems clear that Harman and others who have claimed to find a sense of *ought* in which it expresses a property of an agent have been looking beyond this possibility. This possibility exists generally for the propositional operator, whatever other, lexical, distinctions may be drawn among occurrences of that operator. Harman should rather be understood as claiming that there is at least one use of *ought* which both can be distinguished on lexical grounds and also should *not* be read as a propositional operator. He claims that a use of *ought* which satisfies these conditions is that in which it expresses moral obligation.

I shall first consider the claim about moral obligation, and shall argue that there is no reason to regard the *ought* of moral obligation as anything but a propositional operator. What we need to do, rather than introduce a difference of logical form, is to distinguish between different kinds of states of affairs that ought to be the case, and between different ways in which it can come about that things ought to be the case. I shall later distinguish an *ought* different from that of moral obligation, but this will still not import a difference of logical form.

Consider the pair

(5) Someone ought to help that old lady

and

(6) Jones ought to help that old lady.

A claim such as (6) may, very familiarly, be supported by the claim (5), together with some consideration which specially selects Jones; for instance, that he is the only person within striking distance competent to give the required help. The occurrence of *ought* in (5) is as a propositional operator, and it is hard to see what requires it, or even allows it, to turn into something else in (6). (6) expresses what many people have wanted to call, if perhaps in a broad sense, a moral obligation.

There could be a different kind of reason which supported (6), a reason which started from Jones: as, for instance, that he promised to help her when she needed it, or, again, that he is her nephew. In such a case, we speak in the strictest and least technical sense of Jones being under a moral obligation to help her. That, equally, will be expressed by the sentence (6), and I can see no reason for holding that, as occurring in these two different contexts, it has a different structure. The point that if (6) is indeed of the form '$O(p)$', then it must sustain the active/passive transform, can, it seems to me, merely be accepted for both these contexts. If it is the case that Jones ought to help the lady because Jones is under an obligation to do that, then it does logically follow that the old lady ought to be helped by Jones (it is worth noticing that it does not follow, though it may well be correct, that she ought to be helped by Jones rather than by, for instance, you, who are (say) nearer but under no special obligation to her). Of course it does not follow that she is *under an obligation* to be helped by Jones: not that that is impossible (she might rashly have promised the importunate Jones to accept his offers of help), but because that would follow from a special fact about her, and not from a special fact about Jones. The reason why, in Harman's original example, (1) is 'appropriate' rather than (2) in the obligation case is then fairly obvious. The choice of (1) rather than of (2) suggests that the situation *is* indeed one of obligation, and of an obligation which is Jones'.

If this is right, obligation does not require a new logical structure for *ought* sentences, but only a special kind of reason why it ought to be the case that someone do a particular action. However, it may be argued that this is a superficial suggestion and that when the idea is examined more closely, obligation will, after all, turn out to require the introduction of *ought* as something other than a propositional operator. Let us take the particular case of promising. If A promises to do X, he puts himself under an obligation to do X, and so he ought to do X; that is to say, in the structure so far accepted, O (A does X). But will just any doing of X by A constitute his doing what he ought to do? Clearly not just *any* doing of X by A: at the very least, it is required that A should do X intentionally. But it can be argued that more than this is required, and that if A does what he ought to do, then he must not only do X intentionally, but must do X from a specific motive, namely from the thought that he ought to do X. We might call this the 'Kantian Requirement'. If we accept this Kantian Requirement, then we do need another semantic structure. For, on the present proposal, the notion of A's doing precisely what he ought to do can be represented only as the coming about of precisely that state of affairs which ought to come about; but if the Kantian Requirement holds, then we cannot determinately specify in such a case what state of affairs it is that ought to come about, since the agent's thought has to be part of that state of affairs, and when we come to specify that thought, the question arises again, and we are involved in an unavoidable regress or indeterminacy.

I think that this argument yields a significant conclusion, but that it does not succeed in overthrowing the idea of the unitary structure of *ought*, so far as the present considerations have gone. It is anyway not totally clear to what extent a requirement of the Kantian kind on the agent's motivating thought does actually hold in such cases. To the extent that it does, however, the point will be met by the consideration that the required motivation need not involve a thought which irreducibly introduces a general *ought*. Rather, if such a condition holds on someone carrying out his promises, then what ought to be the case is that A intentionally do X from the thought *that he promised*; and similar considerations apply to other specific forms of obligation. (In fact, it may turn out – though this needs further investigation – that this account of the matter is independently motivated, as giving a coherent account of what exactly it is that people learn when they learn such things as the rule that they ought to keep their promises.)

It is very important that if one agrees that one does not need to go beyond '*O* (*A* does *X*)' to express what follows from *A*'s being under an obligation, one is not thereby committed to the substitution of a consequentialist view for a deontological view. If *A* ought to keep his promise, then the analysis gives us that it ought to be the case that he keep it – that is (if you like), that a certain state of affairs should come about. But we are not committed by that to supposing that this is so because of anything associated with his keeping his promise other than its being a case of his keeping his promise. The consequentialist and similar issues do not concern the merits of the analysis in terms of '*O*(*p*)'. They concern the relation of '*O* (*A* keeps his promise)' to '*O*(*p*)', for some other '*p*'.[2] It might indeed be odd if there were nothing to be said about promise-keeping and its merits beyond the consideration that promises are promises, but that is for reasons that do not follow merely from this analysis.

We shall come back later to some further questions about moral obligation. First, however, we must consider the question of *ought* as it occurs in the deliberative question 'What ought I to do?' There do seem to be considerations which provide a good case for distinguishing such a 'practical' *ought* from the general propositional *ought*. One reason that has been given[3] for making such a distinction is that the practical *ought* is heavily governed by actual reality, whereas the general propositional *ought* is permitted to be adapted to speaker's whim. So '*A* ought to do *X*' (practical) does imply that it is possible that *A* do *X*; in general, however, '*O* (*A* does *X*)' does not – if it is not possible that *A* do *X*, then all the speaker has to concede is that it ought to be the case that it be possible that *A* do *X*. Now the mere fact that the *ought* of deliberation implies possibility certainly does not in itself deliver a distinction of logical form, in particular the distinction between a propositional operator and an *ought* expressing a relational property of the agent. Even where it is unquestionable that the propositional form is being used, differing implications of possibility can be found, which can be readily ascribed to context, purpose of discourse, and similar pragmatic considerations. Thus

(7) This place ought to be a railway station,
said of St Peter's as an aesthetic comment, is not a remark to which

---

[2] cf. 'A Critique of Utilitarianism' in Smart and Williams, *Utilitarianism: For and Against* (Cambridge, 1973), pp. 83–5, on the formality of the concept 'state of affairs' in these connections.

[3] By Bruce Vermazen, 'The Logic of Practical "Ought" Sentences', *Philosophical Studies*, 32 (1977), pp. 1–71.

'it can't be' is a relevant answer; on the other hand, that is a relevant answer to

(8) This space ought to be used for a store

when that is said by the consultant to the management. But (7) and (8) should surely be treated as having the same logical form. If it is correct to regard the *ought* which occurs in statements of moral obligation as being the propositional operator, something similarly pragmatic will have to be said about the application of '*ought* implies *can*' to moral obligation. This is one of the points I shall return to.

There is another[4] feature of the practical *ought* which it certainly does not share with the general propositional *ought*, nor, in my view, with that of moral obligation. The practical *ought* is to be taken to be equivalent to the 'all-in' or 'conclusive' answer to the question 'What ought I to do?', and an *ought* which has that role will have a property which we might call that of being 'exclusive': if I ought to do X and also I ought to do Y, then it must be possible that I can do both X and Y. This is intimately connected with the consideration that the process of deliberation itself involves narrowing down, by rejection, the answers to 'What ought I to do?'

In this use (unlike, I have argued, the case of moral obligation), the application of the active/passive transform does seem doubtful. Suppose that I need to know the way, and see a likely citizen to ask. I conclude that I ought to ask him the way, but it seems very peculiar to put this conclusion by saying that this citizen ought to be asked the way by me. This might suggest that we are not here dealing with a propositional operator; but that suggestion is misleading, and any explanation that there may be for the active/passive phenomenon will have to be found elsewhere. For consider a joint deliberation, as a result of which a speaker concludes

(9) One of us ought to go and inform the manager.

Keeping constant an interpretation of *ought* in the practical or deliberative sense, (9) still has two readings, and one of them requires the propositional operator.[5] It looks as though we can conclude in

---

[4] It is a further feature, since exclusivity requires not only the principle that *ought* implies *can*, but also what I have elsewhere called the 'agglomeration principle', to the effect that if A ought to do X and also ought to do Y, then A ought to do X and Y. See 'Ethical Consistency' in *Problems of the Self* (Cambridge, 1973).

[5] This was pointed out to me by David Wiggins, who remarked that the point is still clearer with *must* in its practical sense (cf. the following chapter), and that it is reasonable to suppose that *ought* and *must*, in their practical or deliberative senses, should share the same logical form. I am grateful to Wiggins for criticism of an earlier draft of this chapter, which has changed my view on several matters.

general that although *ought* requires various distinctions of sense, those distinctions are not associated with the difference of logical form that has been supposed.

In the practical or deliberative sense, '*A* ought to do *X*' will entail '*A* has a reason to do *X*', in what I have called the 'internal' sense of that claim;[6] the two are, however, not equivalent, since '*A* has a reason to do *X*' is not exclusive. Since '*A* ought to do *X*' in the practical sense is relativised to the agent's set of aims, projects, objectives, etc. (including of course moral and other constraints that *A* may recognise), it follows that if a given claim of this kind is based on the assumption that *A* had a certain objective which he does not have, and if there is no sound deliberative route to that objective from objectives that he does have, then the claim is wrong.

It is an obvious possibility, granted these structures, that an agent may recognise various things that he ought to do in the first, propositional, sense we have distinguished, but nevertheless conclude as a result of his deliberation that he ought not to do any of those things. This is not very surprising. It will also be true, so far as the present analysis is concerned, that an agent can consistently recognise that he is under a moral obligation to do a certain thing, yet conclude in his deliberation that he ought not to do that thing – if any necessary supremacy of moral obligation in deliberation is to be argued for, the argument will have to be supplied separately. It equally follows that, in those cases in which the final *ought* of practical deliberation does coincide with some *ought* of moral obligation which is accepted in the course of that deliberation, it will not merely be a last and decisive iteration of it.

The practical *ought*, then, on the present account, will imply possibility, will be exclusive, and will be relative to the projects of the agent in question. It is obvious, given the function of the all-in *ought* of practical deliberation, why it should have just these features. In all but perhaps one of these respects it differs from the *ought* of moral obligation. Or rather we should say, it differs from that *as such*, for of course in the deliberations of an agent who is morally motivated, or in advice given to such an agent, an *ought* of moral obligation and the practical *ought* will often coincide. Moreover, that must be so, to some considerable extent, if there is to be a working system in which moral considerations have any force. They have force only because a fair proportion of agents a fair proportion of the time grant them force in their deliberations.

[6] See chapter 8, above.

The one characteristic in which statements of moral obligation would be generally agreed to resemble the practical *ought* is with respect to '*ought* implies *can*': obligation implies possibility. It is not at all clear that this is right without qualification, at least with regard to the narrower class of obligations, related to such things as contract and status. In these cases, people are more willing to say on occasion that an agent was under an obligation which he was unable to carry out. The agent himself may have this thought, and it may sometimes be accompanied by the kind of regret which characteristically accompanies cases of irresoluble conflict.[7] What underlies this possibility is that in these cases there is a consideration which selects that particular agent and that particular action independently (to some extent at least) of the possibility of his so acting. It is only to some extent so, since if an impossibility can be foreseen, there can be good reason to say that this promise does not count as a promise, or that this is not, after all, one of the obligations of his role. But if it is not foreseeable or has not been foreseen, and the expectations associated with promises and roles are activated, the customary grounds for the agent's being under an obligation are often thought to be enough for him to be under an obligation, even though he cannot carry that obligation out. The further one gets away from these cases, and the wider one casts the notion of moral obligation, the less room there is for this, since in the cases where there is no formal introduction of the obligation, the act of selecting a given *ought* statement about *A* as expressing a moral obligation of *A*'s *itself involves* considering whether he was in a position to do the action. This is because the category of moral obligation is connected to two notions, themselves connected with each other: the notion of blame, and that of actions in which character is expressed through deliberation. Any set of moral ideas at all requires the latter notion, but it is a more open question whether every moral system requires this notion of blame, and, indeed, the wider notion of moral obligation. Insofar as we do use such notions, however, the important point is that we do not first have a determinate notion of moral obligation (in the wider sense) to which the notions of blame and related reactions are then added. The class of moral obligations in the wider sense just *is* the class of *oughts* about an agent's actions to which blame and similar reactions are added. The conclusion follows, for which I have tried to argue, that 'moral obligation' is not a category of *oughts* picked out by logical form.

[7] Of course, if agglomeration is permitted, conflict cases will themselves be examples of this.

What about agents who are outside the system of beliefs of those who are applying the notion of moral obligation? With regard at least to the contractual cases, there is a sense in which they cannot be totally outside it – if they are, then whatever they say will not count as a contract. But in the case of status, and in the wider sense of 'moral obligation', these moral considerations will be thought (in some kinds of case, at least) to apply to an agent who refuses to respond to them. What weight or content is there in the thought that some obligation *applies* to such an agent?

The statement of obligation certainly *refers* to him, but that obvious truth does not capture the thought. Moreover, if he does not care about these considerations, then the commentators will feel that he ought to care about them. That distinguishes the obligations from some other *oughts* (though not from all others), but it does not ultimately provide any more 'hold' over the agent, since whatever question arises about the first *ought* must also arise about this second one.[8] Beyond those facts, however, there are no more – except the rage, frustration, sorrow, and fear of someone who sees someone else convincedly or blandly doing what the first person morally thinks they ought not to be doing. In some sense, this critic deeply wants this *ought* to stick to the agent; but the only glue there is for this purpose is social and psychological.

It is important that this is so, granted almost any interpretation of '$O(p)$' itself, even the most cognitivist interpretations. This is the right place for the standard emotivist or prescriptivist argument, that even where '$O(p)$' has the particular form '$O(A$ does $X)$', if it just tells one a fact about the universe, one needs some further explanation of why A should take any notice of that particular fact.

There is one, and I think only one, interpretation of 'O (A does $X)$' which might hope in itself to deliver a more intimate connection of A to the truth of this sentence, and that is the sense in which it is taken to express an 'external reason' for A to act.[9] This would seek to 'stick' the *ought* to the agent by presenting him as irrational if he ignored it, in a sense in which he is certainly concerned to be rational. I doubt very much, in fact, whether this proposal does capture what the ordinary moral consciousness wants from the *ought* of moral

---

[8] Vermazen's suggestion (op. cit.) that we should isolate an *ought* which expresses a practical *ought* relative to intentions which ideally the agent would have, seems, so far as this question is concerned, to be marching on the spot.

[9] See chapter 8, above.

obligation, as opposed to something read into it by a rationalistic theoretical construct (it could be — though I doubt it — that this is what Kant wanted of the misleadingly named 'Categorical Imperative'). But if this were what was wanted, there would be good reason to see moral obligation as an illusion, since there is good reason to think that there are no external reasons for action.

10 Practical necessity

Someone deliberating in an everyday situation may conclude that a certain action is one that he must, or has to, do. The Kantian moral agent is someone who is controlled by conceptions of what he must do, and so, in his necessarily exceptional way, is the Sophoclean hero. Those conceptions are closer to one another than is often supposed, and they share a modal notion with everyday deliberation, the notion of practical necessity. That notion deserves more attention than it has received.[1]

It will be best, in fact, to start from *ought*. Whatever other *oughts* there may be,[2] we can recognise the use of the expression in the conclusion of deliberation: 'This is what I ought to do' expresses the agent's recognition of the course of action appropriate, all things considered, to the reasons, motives, and constraints that he sees as bearing on the situation. The sense of that conclusion is what gives the sense to the question it answers, 'What ought I to do?'

Of that conclusive *ought*, it is clear that it is *practical*, in the sense that not only is it concerned with action (as opposed, for instance, to being concerned merely with desirable states of affairs), but the action in question has to be one possible for the agent: here, at any rate, 'ought' does imply 'can'. Such an *ought*, moreover, is *exclusive*, in the sense that if I cannot do both *A* and *B* then it cannot be the case both that I ought to do *A* and that I ought to do *B*.[3]

It will be very obvious that this *ought* has nothing specially to do with moral obligation. The question: 'What ought I to do?' can be asked and answered where no question of moral obligation comes into

---

[1] Peter Winch has helpfully discussed a range of issues in this area. See in particular 'The Universalizability of Moral Judgements', *Monist*, 49 (1965), reprinted in his *Ethics and Action* (London, 1972). See also note 6 below.

[2] For at least one other, see chapter 9, above.

[3] Its being exclusive does not follow immediately from its being practical, in the sense of implying possibility. See chapter 9, p. 119, n. 4.

the situation at all; and when moral obligation does come into the question, what I am under an obligation to do may not be what, all things considered, I ought to do – if only (though this is not the only case) because I can also be under a moral obligation to do some other and conflicting thing.

It is worth mentioning that there are important second- and third-person uses of what is, in effect, this *ought*, in contexts of advice or of discussion about what it is reasonable for an agent to do. So used, this *ought* also reveals itself to be *relative*, in a broad sense, to the projects, motives, and so on of the agent in question. If *A* tells *B* that he ought to do a certain thing, but *A* is under a misapprehension about what *B* basically wants or is aiming at, then *A*'s statement, if it is intended in this sense, must be withdrawn.

Ought is related to *must* as *best* is related to *only*. This seems to be a general feature of these terms, even in contexts which are quite removed from either practical deliberation or morality (such as those in which inferences are expressed). In this connection, Prichard was mistaken when he claimed[4] that the *ought* which was 'hypothetical' on an agent's intentions expressed a necessary means to the agent's reaching his objective. What is charactistically expressed by telling someone that he ought to do *X* if he wants *Y* is that *X* is the best or favoured means to *Y*; if it is the only means to *Y*, then he *must* do it if he wants *Y*.

I shall not try to say anything here about the supposed distinction between categorical and hypothetical imperatives, a topic which has generated an exceptional degree of confusion. All that is needed here is the obvious point that if *A* wants *X*, and if it is true that if he wants *X* he must do *Y*, it does not follow that he must do *Y*; that will follow only if, further, *X* is the thing that he must pursue. So, in the first person: if I conclude that I must do *Y*, then it is because I have come to see not just that it is the only means to some end I have, but that it is the only thing I can do.

However, this raises a difficulty. It is very rarely the case that there is only one thing that I *can* do, and that all the alternative courses of action are – in a phrase which invitingly begs all the questions – *literally* impossible. Usually, the alternatives are vastly more costly, or are excluded by some moral constraint. Various considerations that come

---

[4] *Moral Obligation* (Oxford, 1949), p. 91. Prichard says that 'the thought which we wish to convey' is that if the agent does not do the act in question, his purpose will not be realised; indeed, 'this is what we really mean by our statement'.

into deliberation uniquely single out the preferred course of action; the others being ruled out, one is left, and that is what I must do. The difficulty is that this seems a correct description of *any* deliberation which uniquely selects a course of action – and that is any deliberation which issues in a unique conclusion, that is to say, any deliberation which is successful. So it is obscure why any conclusive practical decision should not be of this form, and so every deliberative *ought* be a *must*. But it is not true that every *ought* is a *must*. Why not?

That question might have had only a rather boring answer: for instance, that *must* is selected when the preferred course of action is very markedly favoured over others, or the weight of reasons overwhelmingly comes down on one side. There are cases in which something like the boring answer is correct. Those are the cases in which a set of objectives or constraints is merely taken for granted, and relative to them, a particular course of action is very clearly singled out; the language of necessity may, further, be particularly appropriate if there is some consideration which ordinarily would have discouraged that action. But, in general, the boring answer is wrong. Necessity is not the same as decisiveness. Nor, any more than in any other field, is it the same as certainty. It may only be after a long and anxious consideration of alternatives that an agent concludes that a certain course is what he has to take, and he can have that belief while remaining uncertain about it, and still very clearly seeing the powerful merits of alternative courses.

The most important point, however, is that it is enough for the boring answer that the set of objectives or constraints which determines the outcome should merely be accepted or taken for granted by the agent as something which, so far as this deliberation is concerned, he does not intend to change. But in the serious cases of practical necessity, in which *must* makes its real point, that is not so. In the serious cases, the notion of necesssity is applied to those constraints and objectives themselves.

The language of rhetoric and deceit illustrates the point. Those who are bargaining, blackmailing or threatening, often say that some inadequate response from the other party 'leaves them with no alternative' to taking unpleasant action. These are simply words, but something is to be learned from what the words are meant to suggest. These people would certainly not make the same point if they merely said that this action was, by a long way, the one that they most favoured. Some notion of impossibility of the alternatives, or of the agent's incapacity, is at work. What he is pretending is what we are trying to locate, and that is something other than the mere decisive weight of one set of reasons.

Any notion of necessity must carry with it a corresponding notion of impossibility, and statements in terms of the one can no doubt be recast in terms of the other, but it can make a difference which of them presents itself first and more naturally. In the case of deliberation, there is a significant distinction between two ways in which necessity may enter the structure of my thought. It may be the case that I conclude that I have to do X, for instance because it is the one item to which I attach overwhelming importance, or because, unless I do it, everything will be ruined. Then, as a consequence of this, Y and Z, alternatives to X, are no longer alternatives – they are things I cannot do. Alternatively, it may be the impossibility that bears the priority. Y and Z, the only alternatives to X, are things that I cannot conceivably do, and are excluded; then consequently, X is what I must, or have to, do.

One point which is implicit in this way of expressing these structures of thought is that there is nothing special about *moral* necessity, in any of the narrower senses of that expression which relates specially to such things as obligation; though there may be a broader sense – an ultimately broad sense, relating to character and action – in which all really serious examples of such necessities are moral necessities. Among the constraints, requirements, and impossibilities which an agent recognises are those that obtain for distinctively moral reasons. In particular, the class of things that he cannot do, come (more or less) what may, includes those things he cannot do to other people, courses which are excluded from his range of alternatives, in virtue of what he sees as those people's rights.

In face of 'I must', the other alternatives are no longer alternatives: they become things one cannot do, as, in the other structure, an alternative was something one could not anyway do, and that consideration *led* to 'I must'. But how can an alternative be, or become, something I cannot do? Here someone will reach for the weapon of distinguishing senses, and will speak of there being two or more senses of 'cannot', that which signifies whatever rejection is embodied in the agent's deliberation, and that which expresses what one 'literally' cannot do. But why should we resort to such a distinction of senses? Why should this kind of *cannot* be anything other than *cannot*? It has, for instance, the central feature that if the agent is right in thinking or concluding that he cannot do a certain thing, then – subject to an important qualification which I shall come back to – he will not do it.

It may be said that this is because the situation involves practical acceptance, not because it involves necessity. Thus if an agent accepts that, in the practical sense, he ought to do X, he will – in general, and leaving aside problems of *akrasia* – do X. But this is because people generally (at least) do what they see most reason to do, and not because of the mere implications of *ought*. Thus an adviser may say that A ought to do X and, at least if the adviser speaks in the mode of relative practical advice, he surely says the same thing as A would say if A said 'I ought to do X', and something that would be contrary to A's saying 'I ought not to do X.' But clearly 'A ought to do X', even in this relative practical sense, has no predictive implications about what A will do, and if A does something else, the adviser can stick by his original judgement in the form of saying 'A ought to have done X.'

But this precisely brings out a contrast with *must*. There are indeed some significant ambiguities in this area, and some things that an English speaker may mean by 'you cannot' have nothing to do with prediction at all: thus it may mean 'you are not permitted to'. If the agent does what, in this sense, the observer thinks that the agent 'cannot' do, the observer can retain his original opinion. But the situation is different with the necessity of relative practical advice. The most distinctive English formula for that is perhaps 'You will have to' or, indeed, 'You have no alternative.' These formulae, unlike *must*, have a past tense, but it is an impressive fact that their use in the past tense indeed implies that the agent did do the act in question. Nothing stands to the practical *must* as *ought to have* stands to *ought*. The language of other persons, advisers and observers, itself has features that should encourage us to take seriously the idea that the language of practical necessity is not related by a mere pun to the 'literal' uses of *cannot*; the *cannot* of practical necessity itself introduces a certain kind of incapacity.

What I recognise, when I conclude in deliberation that I cannot do a certain thing, is a certain incapacity of mine. I may be able to think of that course of action, but I cannot entertain it as a serious option. Or I can consider it as an option, but not in the end choose it or do it. These incapacities can be recognised also by the observer. The observer can, moreover, recognise a dimension of this sort of incapacity which the agent himself necessarily cannot register in his deliberation:

that the agent could not think of this course of action at all, that it could not occur to him. The agent can, so to speak, edge up to that condition in his deliberation, in dismissing something as 'unthinkable' – but thinking that something is unthinkable is not so direct a witness to its being unthinkable as is being incapable of thinking of it.

I said that there was a qualification to be made to the claim that, if an agent has this kind of incapacity to do X, then he will not do X. What should rather be said is that he will not do it intentionally. The agent who sincerely says that he cannot do a certain thing, or that he must do something else which excludes that thing, cannot mean without qualification, and no more can an observer, that the world will not contain his doing that thing, for it is certainly compatible with the beliefs of both agent and observer that the agent might do the act unintentionally, for instance in ignorance.

It may be this point, if anything, that is meant by contrasting this incapacity with what an agent 'literally' cannot do. What an agent *simply* cannot do, he cannot do even unintentionally, and that presumably extends to everything that he physically cannot do, so long as the physical, as in our present modes of speech, remains contrasted with the psychological. The incapacities we are concerned with here might broadly be labelled 'incapacities of character', though this needs considerable extension and refinement to cover all the cases introduced by the model of deliberation. These incapacities do not extend to the unintentional, and in many of these cases it is possible that the agent should do the act unintentionally, and his so doing will not falsify the claim that he was incapable of it. Of course, if the act seems only superficially to be unintentional, and we believe that it is not an accident relative to the description of the action under which we thought him incapable of it that he did it, then what we believe is that he is really capable of it, though he may not believe that himself.

It might be suggested that a more radical asymmetry can be found between these kinds of incapacities and standard 'physical' incapacities, with respect to the notion of trying; on the ground that if A cannot physically do X, then it follows that if A tried he would fail, whereas this is evidently not true of the cases under consideration, or at least of all of them. But it is simply not correct that this follows from 'A cannot physically do X', since in many cases there is not anything that counts as trying; while if the world were different enough for something to count as A's trying to do X, then perhaps it would also be a world in which he could do X. The most that follows from 'A

cannot do *X*' is that either it is true that if he were to try to do *X* he would fail, or it is impossible that he should try to do *X*, and that disjunction follows equally in the case of the incapacities which are under discussion here.

We are subject to the model that what one can do sets the limits to deliberation, and that character is revealed by what one chooses within those limits, among the things that one can do. But character (of a person in the first instance; but related points apply to a group, or to a tradition) is equally revealed in the location of those limits, and in the very fact that one can determine, sometimes through deliberation itself, that one cannot do certain things, and must do others. Incapacities can not only set limits to character and provide conditions of it, but can also partly constitute its substance.

To arrive at the conclusion that one must do a certain thing is, typically, to make a discovery – a discovery which is, always minimally and sometimes substantially, a discovery about oneself. The context, nevertheless, is one of practical reasoning, and that fact, together with the consideration that the incapacities in question are, in a broad sense, incapacities of character, will help to explain the important fact that this kind of incapacity cannot turn away blame. I mentioned before the dishonest use of 'I have no alternative.' Part of its deceitfulness may lie in this, that it carries an implication that the speaker cannot be to blame for what he will now do, since there is only one thing for him to do. But the fact that an agent has come to that point, if he has, is certainly not enough to turn away blame. The incapacities we are considering here are ones that help to constitute character, and if one acknowledges responsibility for anything, one must acknowledge responsibility for decisions and action which are expressions of character – to be an expression of character is perhaps the most substantial way in which an action can be one's own.

Conclusions of practical necessity seriously arrived at in serious matters are indeed the paradigm of what one takes responsibility for. That is connected with the fact that they constitute, to a greater or lesser degree, discoveries about oneself. The thought that leads to them, however, is not for the most part thought about oneself, but thought about the world and one's circumstances. That, though it still needs to be understood in philosophy, is not a paradox: it must be true, not only of practical reasoning but more generally, that one finds out about oneself by thinking about the world that exists independently of oneself. The recognition of practical necessity must involve an understanding at once of one's own powers and incapacities, and of what the world permits, and the recognition of a limit which is neither simply external to the self, nor yet a product of the will, is what can lend a special authority or dignity to such decisions – something that can be heard in Luther's famous saying, for instance, but also, from a world far removed from what Luther, Kant, or we, might call 'duty', in the words of Ajax[5] before his suicide: 'now I am going where my way must go'.[6]

[5] Sophocles *Ajax* 690, translated by John Moore. The Greek exactly catches the nature of the practical necessity, which is in this case utterly personal, by expressing it impersonally – literally, 'for now I am going where it must be gone'.

[6] The importance of distinguishing between *must* and *ought* has been emphasised by Stanley Cavell: see now his *Claim of Reason* (Oxford, 1980). See also Roger Wertheimer, *The Significance of Sense* (Cornell, 1972). Wertheimer further claims that *must* is univocal over its various applications, but this is part of a general theory to the effect that the modals (including *ought*) are univocal, which I do not accept, and which has consequences for *must* quite different from the suggestions made here.

11   The truth in relativism

This chapter tries to place certain issues in the discussion of relativism, rather than to deal with any one of them thoroughly. It is concerned with any kind of relativism, in the sense that the questions raised are ones that should be asked with regard to relativistic views in any area, whether it be the world-views of different cultures, shifts in scientific paradigms, or differences of ethical outlook. A machinery is introduced which is intended to apply quite generally. But the only area in which I want to claim that there is truth in relativism is the area of ethical relativism. This does not mean that I here try to argue against its truth in any other area, nor do I try to pursue any of the numerous issues involved in delimiting the ethical from other areas.

1   Conditions of the problem

(a) There have to be two or more *systems of belief* (Ss) which are to some extent self-contained. No very heavy weight is put on the propositional implications of the term 'belief', nor, still less, is it implied that all relevant differences between such systems (let '$S1$', '$S2$', stand for examples from now on) can be adequately expressed in propositional differences: the extent to which this is so will differ with different sorts of examples. Any application of this structure will involve some degree of idealisation, with regard to the coherence and homogeneity of an S. There is more than one way in which these characteristics may be imposed, however, and difference in these affects the way (perhaps, the sense) in which the resultant S is an idealisation.

The characteristics may be involved in the very identification of the Ss: thus two synchronously competing scientific theories may be picked out in part in terms of what bodies of beliefs hang together. But even in this case the Ss will not just be intellectual items constructed from the outside on the basis of the harmony of their content: there will in fact be bodies of scientists working within these theories (or research programmes) and seeking to impose coherence on them. If failures in imposing coherence were to be regarded as *a priori* impossible, the structure of description in terms of various Ss would lose a great deal of explanatory value.

In the case of alien cultures, the identification of an S may be effected initially through other features (geographical isolation and internal interaction of a group of persons), and the coherence of the S operate rather as an ideal limit for the understanding of the group's beliefs. This idea is in fact problematical, at least if taken as indicative of understanding in any objective sense: one comprehensible, and surely plausible, hypothesis is that no group of human beings will have a belief system which is fully coherent. The demand operates, nevertheless, as a constraint on theory-construction about the group, since the data will even more radically underdetermine theory if room is left for indeterminate amounts of incoherence within the S that theory constructs.

The problems of relativism concern communication between $S1$ and $S2$, or between them and some third party, and, in particular, issues of preference between them. It is worth noticing that quite a lot is taken for granted in the construction of the problem-situation already, in the application of the idea of there being a plurality of different Ss. Thus it is presupposed that persons within each S can understand other persons within that S; also that persons receive information in certain ways and not others, are acculturated in certain ways, etc. It may be that some forms of relativism can be shown to be false by reference to these presuppositions themselves: not on the ground (which would prove nothing) that the *genesis* of ideas such as 'a culture', like that of 'relativism' itself, lies in a certain sort of culture, but on the ground that the *application* of a notion such as 'a culture' presupposes the instantiation in the subject-matter of a whole set of relations which can be adequately expressed at all only via the concepts of one culture rather than another (e.g., certain notions of causality). Any relativism which denied the non-relative validity of concepts involved in setting up its problem at all, would be refuted. This aspect of the matter has received some attention;[1] I shall not try to take it further here.

---

[1] See *e.g.*, Steven Lukes, 'Some Problems about Rationality', *European Journal of Sociology* 8 (1967), reprinted in B. R. Wilson ed., *Rationality*, Oxford, 1970; and 'On the Social Determination of Truth', in R. Horton and R. Finnegan eds., *Modes of Thought*, London, 1973.

(b) S_1 and S_2 have to be *exclusive of one another*. That this should in some sense be so is a necessary condition of the problems arising to which relativism is supposed to provide an answer; indeed, it can itself be seen as a condition of identifying S_1 and S_2, in any sense relevant to those problems. Suppose for example that two putative Ss constituted merely the history or geography of two different times or places: then evidently they are not Ss in the sense of the problem, because they can merely be conjoined.

A much harder question, however, is raised by asking what are the (most general) conditions of two Ss excluding one another. The most straightforward case is that in which S_1 and S_2 have conflicting consequences, a condition which I shall first take in the form of requiring that there be some yes/no question to which consequence C_1 of S_1 answers 'yes' and consequence C_2 of S_2 answers 'no'. Under this condition, S_1 and S_2 have to be (at least in the respect in question) *comparable*.

The questions to which relativism is supposed to give an answer may be raised by the case of conflicting consequences, but relativism will not stay around as an answer to them unless something else is also true, namely that the answering of a yes/no question of this sort in one way rather than the other does not constrain either the holder of S_1 or the holder of S_2 to abandon respectively the positions characteristic of S_1 and S_2 (and of the difference between them). If this further condition does not hold, there will be a straightforward decision procedure between S_1 and S_2, and relativism will have been banished. In the scientific case, the possibility of this condition holding, granted that C_1 and C_2 are consequences of S_1 and S_2, lies in the possibility that the consequence follows from the system only using material peripheral to the system and to its most characteristic positions: the situation is the much-discussed one in which theory is underdetermined by observation.

However, if theory is radically underdetermined by observation, can it be required that Ss are even to this modest degree comparable? Thus, in the spirit of one fashionable line of argument, if every observation statement is theory-laden, and all theory-ladenness displays meaning-variance, then it is unclear how there can be one yes/no question which stands in the required relation to S_1 and S_2. Here it is important to see how little is implied by there being conflicting consequences of S_1 and S_2. All that is required is that there be *some* description of a possible outcome, which description is acceptable to both S_1 and S_2, and in

terms of which a univocal yes/no question can be formed: it may well
be that there are other descriptions of what is (in some sense) the same
event which are non-comparable. If this minimal requirement is not
satisfied, severe problems are likely to follow, particularly in the case
of scientific theories, for the original description of the Ss. We lose
control on the notion of observation, concerning which it is said that
it underdetermines theory; and we lose the descriptions of certain
passages in the history of science which are the subject and in some
part the motivation of these accounts (roughly it looks as though not
only the choice of a replacement paradigm, but the occasion of
that choice, might emerge as entirely socially determined, as though
a chief determinant of the alteration of scientific theory were
boredom.)

However it may be with scientific theories, it would be unwise to
exclude the possibility of systems so disparate that they were not, in
terms of conflicting consequences, comparable at all. Some social
anthropologists have given accounts of the Ss of traditional (pre-
scientific) societies in terms which seem to imply that they are quite
incommensurable with the Ss of modern, scientific, societies. I shall
not go into the question of whether such accounts could be true.[2] The
issue is rather, if such accounts were true, what content could be left
to the idea that the traditional and the scientific Ss were exclusive of
one another – as surely everyone, including these social anthropologists, would say that they were. Here it looks as though the only thing
to be said is that, in ways which need to be analysed, it is impossible to
live within both Ss. Accepting this vague idea, we can indeed continue
to use, at a different level, the language of conflicting consequences,
since if it is impossible to live within both S_1 and S_2, then the
consequences of (holding) S_1 include actions, practices, etc. which are
incompatible with those which are consequences of (holding) S_2.

I do not take this to be a very illuminating assimilation, since the
variation required in the interpretation of 'consequence' remains
unexplained. But it does harmlessly help to handle a wider range of
cases without constant qualification; and it does, more than that,
positively bring out one thing – that even in this limiting case (which
I shall call that of *incommensurable exclusivity*), there has to be something
which can be identified as the *locus* of exclusivity, and hence the Ss
are not entirely incommensurable. This locus will be that of

---

[2] For an illuminating discussion, see Robin Horton, 'Lévy-Bruhl, Durkheim and the
Scientific Revolution', in Horton and Finnegan eds. op cit.

the actions or practices which are the consequences of living within S_1 and S_2. Another light will be shed on them when we turn, next, to broadly ethical cases.

In ethical cases (taken in a broad sense), the conditions of conflict come out, obviously enough, differently from the form they take with, for instance, scientific theories. The simplest case is that of conflict between answers which are given to yes/no questions which are practical questions, questions about whether to do a certain thing. Now such a question might be a general, or type, action question, asking whether a certain type of thing was to be done in a certain type of situation. In this case, the relevant formulation is that it is possible for S_1 to answer 'yes' to such a question while S_2 answers 'no' to it; this is parallel to two theories yielding conflicting predictions, but without the question yet being raised of one or the other actually being borne out in fact. We get a structure resembling the occurrence of an actual observation only when we move to the idea of a particular token action question, as asked by a particular agent in a particular situation. Here the practical question *gets answered* in actual fact, and this occurrence of course trivially satisfies the conditions: the fact that a given question gets answered in this sense in a way which conflicts with, say, the consequence of S_1 does not constrain a holder of S_1 to abandon his position (he may say that the agent was wrong so to decide). What actually is done trivially underdetermines systems of belief about what ought to be done.

Action decisions are not the only possible site of conflicting consequences in the ethical case: various forms of approval, sentiment, etc. can equally come into it. With these, but also with action-descriptions, difficulties can, once more, arise about the satisfaction of the comparability condition. This condition is easily satisfied under a theory such as Hare's, which is strongly analogous to a positivist philosophy of science, in regarding an ethical outlook or value system (theory) as consisting of a set of principles (laws) whose content is totally characterised by what imperatives (predictions) they generate. But on any more complex view, very severe problems of comparability arise. Here again, we can appeal to the weak requirement which was made in the theory case: that there be some description of the action (say) in terms of which a univocal yes/no question can be formulated. Thus it is certainly true and important that marriage to two persons in a polygamous society is not the same state or action as bigamy in a monogamous society, nor is human sacrifice the same action as murder in the course of armed robbery. But there may well be descriptions such that a univocal yes/no question can be formed for each of these examples, and $S1$ and $S2$ differ in their answers. There can be, that is to say, system-based conflict. Two persons can be in a situation of conflict, in which they give opposed answers to the same question of action or approval, and they can be motivated to this by their value system (that is to exclude quarrels inspired by motivations themselves not sanctioned by the value system).

The line I have sketched for describing cases (if there are any) of incommensurable exclusivity implies that for every pair of Ss which are incommensurably exclusive, there must be some action, practice, etc., which under some agreed description will be a locus of disagreement between the holders of the Ss. If this condition is not met, it is unclear what room is left for the notion of exclusivity at all, and hence for the problems of relativism.

2 Variation and confrontation

With regard to a given kind of S, there can be both diachronic and synchronic variation. In the history and philosophy of science, anthropology, etc., there is room for a great deal of discussion about the interrelations of and the limitations of these kinds of variation. There is for instance the question whether certain synchronic variations represent certain diachronic ones, i.e., whether certain cultural variations in one place are survivals of what was an earlier culture elsewhere (do the Hottentots have a Stone Age culture?). Again, the definition of a certain class of Ss can limit variation: thus the range within which something can count as a *scientific theory* is a well-known matter of dispute, as is the question whether the use of such restrictions to delimit what is counted as diachronic variation (to constitute, that is, a history *of science*) is merely a matter of *ex post facto* evaluation. (The matter takes on a different aspect with respect to synchronic variation at the present time, in view of the existence of a unified and institutionalized international scientific culture.)

In many, if not all, cases of diachronic variation, it is an important fact that a later S involves consciousness of at least its neighbouring predecessor (though not necessarily, of course, in terms which the predecessor, or again S's successors, would assent to). There are very important issues at this point about the writing of 'objective' cultural history, but I do not intend to take them on. In fact, I propose from this point on to ignore cases in which S2 arises in a way which involves some conscious relation with S1, and to consider only those in which mutual awareness can be regarded as, in principle, a development independent of the existence of S1 and S2. While this simplification is a drastic one, it will do for present purposes.

Under this simplification, let us now consider some possible relations, or lack of them, between S1 and S2. There is, first, the primitive situation in which S1 and S2 exist in ignorance of one another. After that, there are cases in which at least one of S1 and S2 encounters the other: either directly, in the case in which persons who hold one of the Ss encounter persons who hold the other, or indirectly, when persons holding one merely learn of the other.

Some such encounters, I shall call *real confrontations* (the term 'confrontation' is not meant to carry all the implications it has in contemporary politics). For any S, there has to be something which counts as assenting to that S, fully accepting it or living within it – whatever it is, in each sort of case, for an S of that sort to be *somebody's* S. I shall call this relation in general 'holding'. There is a real confrontation between S1 and S2 at a given time if there is a group at that time for whom each of S1 and S2 is a real option. This includes, but is not confined to, the case of a group which already holds S1 or S2, for whom the question is one of whether to *go over* to the other S. We shall come back shortly to the question of what a 'real option' is.

Contrasted with this situation is that of *notional confrontation.*[3] Notional confrontation resembles real confrontation in that there are persons who are aware of S1 and S2, and aware of their differences; it differs from it in that at least one of S1 and S2 do not present a real option to them. S1 and S2 can of course be in both real and notional confrontation, but not with respect to the same persons at the same time. S1 and S2 can be in notional confrontation without ever having been in real confrontation: no-one may come to know of both S1 and S2 until at least one of them has ceased to present real options. Again, S1 and S2 can be in real confrontation without ever being in notional confrontation: no-one may ever think of one of them after the hour of its struggle (presumably unsuccessful) with the other.

What is it for an S to be a real option? In accordance with the

[3] The terminology of 'real' and 'notional' was suggested by Newman's *Grammar of Assent.*

starting-point that Ss belong to groups (which is not to deny that they are held by individuals, but to assert that they are held by individuals in ways which require description and explanation by reference to the group), the idea of a real option is meant to be a social notion. S2 is a real option for a group if either it is their S or it is possible for them to go over to S2; where going over to S2 involves, first, that it is possible for them to live within, or hold, S2 and retain their hold on reality, and, second, to the extent that rational comparison between S2 and their present outlook is possible, they could acknowledge their transition to S2 in the light of such comparison.[4] Both these conditions use concepts which imply that whether a given S is a real option to a given group at a given time is, to some extent at least, a matter of degree: this consequence is not unwelcome.

Something must be said in explanation of each of these conditions. Let me take the second first. The purpose of this is to ensure that the question of whether an S is a real option is not just (granted the satisfaction of the first condition) a matter of such things as the state of psychological technology. We do not want to say that an eccentric scientific theory is a real option for a group of scientists because they could be drugged or operated upon in such a way that they emerged believing it. To the extent that S1 and S2 are comparable, do expose themselves to experiment which can tend to favour one over the other, etc., these methods of assessment are what are to count in the consideration of the accessibility of S2 from S1. Whether something is a real option is a social question, but one rooted in as much rationality as is available on the given type of issue.

In the limiting case of incommensurable exclusivity, this condition will have virtually no effect. There will be little room in such a case for anything except conversion. But even conversion had better be something which can be lived sanely, and this is the force of the first condition. To speak of people who have accepted S2 'retaining their hold on reality' is to imply such things as that it is possible for S2 to become their S, and for them to live within S2, without their engaging in extensive self-deception, falling into paranoia, and such things. The extent to which that is so depends in turn, to some degree, on what features of their existing social situation are held constant under the

4 'They' does not mean 'each and every one of them': the problem is a familiar one in the description of social phenomena. There are other difficulties which will have to be overlooked, connected with the very simple use made of the notion of a group – e.g., that it ignores the case of persons who could adopt a different S if they belonged to a different group.

assumption of their going over to $S2$. Thus $S2$ may not be realistically possible for a group granted features of their present social situation, but it might be if those features were changed. The question of whether $S2$ is, after all, a real option for them then involves the question of whether those features could be changed.

It is neither a necessary nor a sufficient condition of an S's being a real option for a group that they think that it is a real option. It is not a sufficient condition, because they may be ill-informed, unimaginative, un-self-aware or optimistic about what it would be like for them to try to live within that S (and this may not be just a personal, but a social or political mistake). It is not a necessary condition, because they may not have realised what possibilities going over to that S would offer them: the psychology of conversion of course relates to this matter. I regard the question of whether a given S is a real option for a given group at a given time as basically an objective question. Of course, people may differ about such questions as what is included under 'a hold on reality', and also, notoriously, about what degree of rational comparability can be displayed by Ss of a given kind. In terms of the present structure, such disagreements may well affect what range of Ss those people will regard as real options, for themselves or others.

In this sense many Ss which have been held are not real options now. The life of a Greek Bronze Age chief, or a mediaeval Samurai, and the outlooks that go with those, are not real options for us: there is no way of living them. This is not to say that reflection on those value-systems may not provide inspiration for thoughts about elements missing from modern life, but there is no way of taking on those Ss. Even Utopian projects among a small band of enthusiasts could not reproduce *that* life. Still more, the project of re-enacting it on a societal scale in the context of actual modern industrial life would involve one of those social or political mistakes, in fact a vast illusion. The prospect of removing the conditions of modern industrial life altogether is something else again – another, though different, impossibility.

In this connexion it is important that there are asymmetrically related options. Some version of modern technological life and its outlooks has become a real option for members of some traditional societies, but their life is not, despite the passionate nostalgia of many, a real option for us. The theories one has about the nature and extent of such asymmetries (which Hegelians would ground in asymmetries of both history and consciousness) affect one's views about the objective possibilities of radical social and political action.

3   Relativism

Suppose that we are in real confrontation with some S. Then there will be some vocabulary of appraisal – 'true–false', 'right–wrong', 'acceptable–unacceptable' etc. – which will be deployed, and essentially deployed, in thought and speech about this confrontation. The ways in which it is deployed, and the considerations it is geared into, will of course differ with the type of S in question – for instance, with the degree of comparability that obtains between Ss of this type. Whatever these differences, in speaking of a 'vocabulary of appraisal', I refer only to those expressions which can *at least* be used to express one's own acceptance or rejection of an S or an element of an S. Such a vocabulary is essentially deployed in reflective thought within situations of real confrontation, since in reflection one has to be able to think, and articulate one's feelings, about the different Ss which are a real option for one, and to organise what is to be said in favour or against a given S becoming one's own. Since Ss are things held or accepted, not just conformed to, what has to be said in favour of or against a given S must have some footing in the appraisal of its content.

We can also use this vocabulary about Ss which stand in merely notional confrontation with our own. For some types of S, however, the life of the vocabulary is largely confined to cases of real confrontation, and the more remote a given S is from being a real option for us, the less substantial seems the question of whether it is 'true', 'right', etc. While the vocabulary can no doubt be applied without linguistic impropriety, there is so little to this use, so little of what gives content to the appraisals in the context of real confrontation, that we can say that for a reflective person the question of appraisal does not genuinely arise for such a type of S when it is standing in purely notional confrontation.

We can register that the S in question is not ours, and that it is not a real option for us. There is indeed quite a lot we can say about it, and relevantly to our concerns. Thus certain features of an alien way of life, for instance, can stand to us symbolically as emblems of conduct and character to which we have certain attitudes in our own society, in much the same way, indeed, as we can treat works of fiction. The socially and historically remote has always been an important object of self-critical and self-encouraging fantasy. But from the standpoint I am now considering, to raise seriously questions in the vocabulary of appraisal about this culture considered as a concrete historical reality will not be possible for a reflective person. In the case of such Ss, to stand in merely notional confrontation is to lack the relation to our concerns which alone gives any point or substance to appraisal. With them, the only real questions of appraisal are about real options.

To think that the standpoint I have just sketched is the appropriate standpoint towards a given type of Ss is, in a recognizable sense, to hold a relativistic view of such Ss. Relativism, with regard to a given type of S, is the view that for one whose S stands in purely notional confrontation with such an S, questions of appraisal of it do not genuinely arise. This form of relativism, unlike most others,[5] is coherent. The truth in relativism – which I shall state, not argue for – is that for ethical outlooks at least this standpoint is correct.

This form of relativism (as a structure – its application to any particular type of S will always of course be a further question) is coherent because unlike most other forms it manages, in the distinction between real and notional confrontation, to cohere with two propositions both of which are true. The first is that we must have a form of thought not relativized to our own existing S for thinking about other Ss which may be of concern to us, and to express those concerns. The second is that we can nevertheless recognize that there can be many Ss which are related to our concerns too distantly for our judgments to have any grip on them, while admitting that other persons' judgment might get a grip on them, namely, those for whom they were a real option.

Most traditional forms of relativism have paid insufficient respect to the first of these propositions. The simplest form merely seeks to relativize the vocabulary of appraisal, into such phrases as 'true for us', 'true for them'. It is well known that these formulations do not work, and in particular cannot represent the basic use of the vocabulary in real confrontations. This view could be said to reduce the entire vocabulary of appraisal to expressions for the description of confrontation. Related to this is the view in ethics which I have elsewhere[6] called 'vulgar relativism', the view which combines a relativistic account of the meaning or content of ethical terms with a non-relativistic principle of toleration. This view is not hard to refute; it was perhaps worth discussing, since it is widely held, but to dispose of it certainly does not take us very far. We can perhaps now see that view more

---

[5] For a different kind of relativist view which avoids the standard errors, see Gilbert Harman, 'Moral Relativism Defended', *Philosophical Review* 84 (1975), pp. 3–22.

[6] *Morality* (Harmondsworth, 1972), ch. 3.

clearly. What vulgar relativism tries to do is to treat real confrontations like notional confrontations, with the result that it either denies that there are any real confrontations at all, or else brings to bear on them a principle which is inadequate to solve them, and is so because while it looks like a principle for deciding between real options, it is really an expression of the impossibility or pointlessness of choosing between unreal options.

Opposed to these kinds of views is that which represents the use of the vocabulary of appraisal as solely that of expressing (not stating) that an *S* is or is not the speaker's own. For such a view (consider for example the pure redundancy or 'speech-act' view of 'true') the issues which have concerned relativists evaporate – there is no way of expressing them. But equally, what has rightly concerned relativists evaporates, and we lose hold on the second truth which the present account is designed to accommodate. The distinction among *S*s, between that which is and those which are not the speaker's own, is by no means the most significant in this area. The assumption that it is, is something that the discarded forms of relativism, and the evaporating view which apparently stands opposed to them, have in common.

With those types of *S* for which relativism is not true, it is not that there is no distinction between real and notional confrontations, but that questions of appraisal genuinely arise even for *S*s in notional confrontation. But if that is so, then the status of those *S*s will reveal itself also in the relevant criteria for distinguishing real and notional confrontations, the considerations that go into determining that a given *S* is or is not a real option for a given group at a given time. This is important for the case of scientific theories. Phlogiston theory is, I take it, not now a real option, but I doubt that this just means that to try to live the life of a convinced phlogiston theorist in the contemporary Royal Society is as incoherent an enterprise as to try to live the life of a Teutonic knight in 1930s Nuremberg. One reason that phlogiston theory is not a real option is that it cannot be squared with a lot that we know to be true.

These considerations, if pursued, would lead us to the subject of realism. One necessary (but not sufficient) condition of there being the kind of truth I have tried to explain in relativism as applied to ethics, is that ethical realism is false, and there is nothing for ethical *S*s to be true of – though there are things for them to be true to, which is why many options are unreal. But scientific realism could be true, and if it is, relativism for scientific theories must be false.

[margin annotation: e.g. scientific theories]

12   Wittgenstein and idealism

1   *Solipsism and the* Tractatus

Tractatus 5.62 famously says: 'what the solipsist *means* is quite correct;
only it cannot be *said* but makes itself manifest. The world is *my* world:
this is manifest in the fact that the limits of *language* (of that language
which alone I understand) mean the limits of my world.' The later
part of this repeats what was said in summary at 5.6: 'the limits of
my language mean the limits of my world'. And the key to the
problem 'how much truth there is in solipsism' has been provided by
the reflections of 5.61:

Logic pervades the world; the limits of the world are also its limits.

So we cannot say in logic 'the world has this in it, and this, but not that'.

For that would appear to presuppose that we were excluding certain
possibilities, and this cannot be the case, since it would require that logic
should go beyond the limits of the world; for only in that way could it view
those limits from the other side as well.

We cannot think what we cannot think; so we cannot think what we
cannot *say* either.

Now Wittgenstein says that 'there is no such thing as the self that thinks
and entertains ideas' (5.631), and this item is presumably the same as
what at 5.641 he perhaps loosely, but comprehensibly, calls 'the human
soul with which psychology deals' – that is to say, the item that does
not really exist, the thinking and knowing soul *in* the world, is an item
which people look for there as the subject of the phenomena with
which psychology deals. In this interpretation I think I am substantially
in agreement with P. M. S. Hacker in his book *Insight and Illusion:
Wittgenstein on Philosophy and the Metaphysics of Experience* (OUP,
1972), which I have found helpful on these questions. There are,
however, respects in which I would put the position rather differently
from him. Hacker, as against Black and others, says that what

Wittgenstein does is to deny the existence of a knowing self *in* the world, and denies it, moreover, on Humean grounds[1] to the effect that it cannot be encountered in experience. At the same time, Wittgenstein, under Schopenhauerian influence, does believe in the existence of another, metaphysical or philosophical self, which is 'the limit of the world, not a part of it' (5.632, 5.641), and in some such sense he really is a solipsist; only that of course cannot be said, but merely manifests itself. Since Wittgenstein denies the first of these selves and in some way or other accepts the second, he cannot mean them to be the same thing.

Granted the intensely paradoxical and ironical character of Wittgenstein's thought here, one is in any case in expounding it going to be choosing between different kinds of emphasis. But I would enter two qualifications to Hacker's account. First, as regards the negative movement against the knowing self, it is not just an unsuccessful Humean search that we are dealing with. Wittgenstein says:

There is no such thing as the subject that thinks or entertains ideas.

If I wrote a book called *The World as I Found It*, I should have to include a report on my body, and should have to say which parts were subordinate to my will, and which were not, etc., this being a method of isolating the subject, or rather of showing that in an important sense there is no subject; for it alone could not be mentioned in that book. (5.631)

He adds, just before the analogy of the visual field, which I shall not consider (5.633): 'where *in* the world is a metaphysical subject to be found...?' This seems to me to say, not just that there was something we were looking for and which turned out not in fact to be in the world – which is Hume's tone of voice, though the full content of Hume's negative discovery is not to be found in his failing to find something which he might have found, either. Rather Wittgenstein says: that which I confusedly had in mind when I set out to look is something which could not possibly be in the world. Hacker's emphasis is: there is one specification, which is the specification of a possible empirical thing, and to that nothing as a matter of fact corresponds; but there is a quasi-specification of a non-empirical thing to which something does, in a way, correspond. But rather, what we first looked for was never a possible empirical thing. For it had to satisfy the condition of being something *in* the world as I experience it and yet at the same time necessarily there whenever anything was there,

---

[1] Hacker, p. 59.

and there could not be anything which did that. This is why Wittgenstein can explain his thought in this connection by saying (5.634) that no part of our experience is at the same time *a priori* (the phrase translated 'at the same time' is important here). Thus Wittgenstein's thought is, as Hacker indeed says, very like Kant's criticism of the Cartesian *res cogitans*.

The other qualification affects the other half of the argument. We cannot in any straightforward sense say that there is, or that we can believe in, or accept, a metaphysical, transcendental, self instead; for neither *what* it is, nor *that* it is, can be said, and attempts to talk about it or state its existence must certainly be nonsense. That is why, as we have already seen, the non-occurrence of a subject in the book of *The World as I Found It* means that 'in an important sense there is no subject'. The sense in which it *is* a limit, also means that *at* the limit, it is not anything at all (5.64):

Here it can be seen that solipsism, when its implications are followed out strictly, coincides with pure realism. The self of solipsism shrinks to a point without extension and there remains the reality co-ordinated with it.

Indeed, granted this, I find puzzling why Wittgenstein can say (5.641) that there really is a sense in which philosophy can talk about the self in a non-psychological way. But I take this to mean that philosophy can talk about it in the only way in which by the end of the *Tractatus*, we find that *philosophy* can talk about anything: that is to say, not with sense.

Whatever exactly we make of that, we can recover from the *Tractatus* discussion of the self and solipsism three ideas which will be particularly important as points of reference in what follows: that the limits of my language are the limits of my world; that there could be no way in which those limits could be staked out from both sides – rather, the limits of language and thought reveal themselves in the *fact that* certain things are nonsensical; and (what follows from the first two, but is an important point to emphasise) that the 'me' and 'my' which occur in those remarks do not relate to an 'I' *in* the world, and hence we cannot conceive of it as a matter of empirical investigation (as the *Tractatus* is fond of putting it, a matter of 'natural science') to determine why my world is this way rather than that way, why my language has some features rather than others, etc. Any sense in which such investigations were possible would not be a sense of 'my', or indeed, perhaps, of 'language', in which the limits of my language were the limits of my world.

It may seem that these ideas are foremost among those that Wittgenstein abandoned in his later work, and that they, and the forms of puzzlement which gave rise to them, were particular objects of the criticisms of the *Investigations*. In a sense that is true, and Hacker devotes a good deal of his book to explaining how the later interest in such things as the impossibility of a private language and the necessity for public criteria is related to a long-term project of exorcising solipsism – exorcising it even from some vanishing and unsayable transcendental redoubt. The later arguments about oneself and others are designed (among other things) to remove the need even to try to point, hopelessly, in a solipsistic direction. That need certainly exists in the *Tractatus*. The well-charted moves in the later work from 'I' to 'we' mark one and the most evident attempt to banish that need; equally the emphasis in the later work on language's being an embodied, this-worldly, concrete social activity, expressive of human needs, as opposed to the largely timeless, unlocated and impersonal designatings of the *Tractatus* – that emphasis also can naturally be thought of as a rejection of the transcendental and Schopenhauerian aspects of the earlier work: the *transcendentales Geschwätz*, the 'transcendental twaddle' as Wittgenstein wrote to Engelmann in a different context in 1918 (quoted by Hacker, p. 81).

But the question is not as simple as this, and my chief aim will be to suggest that the move from 'I' to 'we' was not unequivocally accompanied by an abandonment of the concerns of transcendental idealism. To some extent, the three ideas I mentioned are not so much left behind, as themselves take part in the shift from 'I' to 'we': *the shift from 'I' to 'we' takes place within the transcendental ideas themselves.* From the *Tractatus* combination (as Hacker justly puts it) of empirical realism and transcendental solipsism, the move does not consist just in the loss of the second element. Rather, the move is to something which itself contains an important element of idealism. That element is concealed, qualified, overlaid with other things, but I shall suggest that it is there. I shall suggest also that this element may help to explain a particular feature of the later work, namely a pervasive vagueness and indefiniteness evident in the use Wittgenstein makes of 'we'.

2 Solipsism and idealism

Hacker says (p. 59) that an aim of his book is 'to show that the detailed refutation of solipsism and hence of idealism, which Wittgenstein produced in the 1930s and incorporated, in low key, in the *Investigations*, is directed against views which he himself held as a young man'. A refutation 'of solipsism and *hence* of idealism': this is a connexion of ideas, not immediately self-evident, which Hacker makes throughout. Thus at p. 214:

> The solipsist claimed that the present moment is unique, that he is privileged, that it is always he who sees, that what he has when he sees is unique, that his seeing is exceptional, that 'this' is incomparable. Each move is illegitimate. The illegitimacy of each move damns not just solipsism, but phenomenalism and indeed any form of idealism.

Yet it is not at all obvious that everything which could pointfully be called a form of idealism, or indeed which has been so called by the history of philosophy, would necessarily be refuted by arguments which, by undermining a private language, removed the supposed privileged first-person immediacies which are the basis of solipsism, whether expressed or presupposed.

To phenomenalism, which Hacker mentions, such criticism can indeed be extended, and it may help towards the business of sketching a kind of idealism to which that criticism does not extend, if we first consider one or two points about phenomenalism. Phenomenalists used stoutly to hold that it was a crass misunderstanding to regard their theory as any form of idealism. If they were right at all in holding that, clearly their denial applies at best only to non-transcendental idealism – which we may call, following Kant, *empirical* idealism, and which we can define for our present purposes as a form of idealism which regards the existence of the material world as dependent on minds which are themselves things *in* the world, empirical beings whose existence or non-existence is a matter of contingent fact.[2]

In fact, it is not clear that phenomenalism even manages to avoid being that. The question of whether it does or not, turns on the issue of the status of the hypothetical observers whose equally hypothetical sense-data constitute the content, under phenomenalist translation, of statements about unobserved portions of the material world. If *they* are regarded as empirical items, then there may be a difficulty about phenomenalism's steering clear of empirical idealism. For if it is to do that, and so maintain its professed stance as a realist theory at the empirical level, then it must be able to translate into its language any

---

[2] This definition excludes Berkeley's completed theory from being an example of empirical idealism. Yet clearly Kant was right in distinguishing Berkeley's views from transcendental idealism. We need not, for the present purpose, pursue the important distinctions which are needed here.

comprehensible *empirical* proposition which denies the mind-dependence of material objects: thus phenomenalists are happy to translate into their language, as they hope, propositions saying that there were rocks, etc. in certain spaces before there were any observers of them. But what about the following proposition, which seems to be a comprehensible and indeed true empirical proposition in the material object language: 'Even if there were not any observers, certain material objects would exist'? If phenomenalist observers are empirical items, the question of their existence is an empirical question – the same empirical question, indeed, as is raised by the antecedent of that conditional. Thus the phenomenalist translation of that conditional must be of the form: if *P* were not the case, then if *P* were the case, then *Q*, and it is not, to say the least of it, clear that that is satisfactory.

If that cannot be made satisfactory, then phenomenalism cannot adequately represent in its terms a proposition which constitutes a basic empirical denial of mind-dependence. It will be thus a form of empirical idealism. But even if we dispose of that, phenomenalism will still be a kind of transcendental idealism. Suppose that we eliminate the antecedents of the phenomenalist sentences which merely hypothesise the existence of observers, and which are there just as a universal condition of the analysis. Thus we make the so-called existence of observers a redundant condition on the occurrence of sense-data. Then genuinely empirical statements about the existence or non-existence of observers, such as the antecedent of the material object statement we considered just now, can be translated into the phenomenalist language: in some such form, presumably, as statements of the existence of Humean aggregations of sense-data. Then the sense-data which are the raw materials of the phenomenalist translations (including those sense-data aggregations of which constitute the empirical existence of observers) will not, as such, have a subject, and it is obvious from what has just been said why they cannot, as such, have a subject. The only candidate for a subject recognisable to phenomenalism will be the empirical observer, but his existence has now been represented as the contingent aggregation of items which already, and even outside such an aggregation, have the character of sense-data. As Carnap said in the *Logische Aufbau*, '*das Gegebene ist subjektlos*', the given has no subject.

But it is still the *given*: and unless phenomenalism is to surrender its basically epistemological way of introducing one to these items, and its references to their being, or being related to, *observations*, they must remain items of which we have been given no adequate grasp unless they are in *some* sense mental. Neutral monism perhaps attempted to drop that implication, but to the limited extent that it progressed in that attempt, it seems not to leave one with any adequate bearings on the items in question at all. But then, while no form of mind-dependence of the world can be truly asserted *in* the phenomenalist language, the fact that its raw materials are of this character, and the fact that it is basically *the* language,[3] these facts *show* that the world is mental. We cannot say (except empirically and falsely) that the world is the world of experience: rather, its being the world of experience conditions everything we say. That is what it is for phenomenalism to be a form of transcendental idealism, a form which indeed is liable to the same objections as Wittgenstein, faced with solipsism, made to such things as the empiricist theory of meaning. Those objections are directed to starting with supposed first-person immediacies, and phenomenalism incurs them because that in terms of which it represents the world cannot be understood except in terms of first-person immediacies.

Thus phenomenalism is one or another form of idealism, and in either form is exposed, as much as solipsism, to the later Wittgenstein arguments. But, to turn away now from phenomenalism, must anything which could be called idealism have this character? Hacker, as I have mentioned, assumes that it is so. His reason for that emerges when he says (p. 216) that 'idealism in most of its forms' – that is his one qualification – is just a half-hearted form of solipsism which has not been thought through with the consistency of solipsism; thus also he refers (p. 71) to Schopenhauer's 'glib dismissal' of solipsism. Idealism is regarded just as a kind of aggregative solipsism. That is indeed ridiculous,[4] but if the idea that the limits of *my* language mean the limits of *my* world can point to transcendental solipsism, then perhaps there is a form of transcendental idealism which is suggested, not indeed by the confused idea that the limits of *each* person's language mean the limits of *each* person's world, but by the idea that the limits of *our* language mean the limits of *our* world. This would not succumb to the arguments which finished off solipsism, for those arguments are all basically about the move from 'I' to 'we', and that, in this version, has already been allowed for.

[3] I shall not try to discuss how that second fact is to be understood. For the closely related point that the 'two languages' version of phenomenalism is not neutral about reality, cf. J. L. Austin, *Sense and Sensibilia* (Oxford, 1962), pp. 60–1.

[4] Cf. Moore's objection to what he supposed to be a consequence of egoism in ethics: *Principia Ethica* (Cambridge, 1903), p. 99.

I think that there is such a view implicit in some of Wittgenstein's later work. To see what such a view will be like, we can try to follow an analogy between this, first-person plural, view, and the first-person singular transcendental view which we have already touched on. First and most basically it is essential that the proposition that the limits of our language mean the limits of our world should be taken neither as a blank tautology, nor as an empirical claim. It would be a mere tautology if it meant something like: whoever are meant by 'we', it is going to be true that what we understand, we understand, and what we have heard of and can speak of, we have heard of and can speak of, and what we cannot speak of, we cannot speak of. Certainly. But the singular versions of those truisms were not just what was meant when it was said originally that the limits of my language meant the limits of my world. Nor, in that original case, did we intend an *empirical* thought, in which I both take myself as something in the world and make it depend on me. That is precisely what we left behind in distinguishing transcendental from empirical idealism. Now, we do not mean the plural analogue of that empirical monomania, either, and that is one way in which our statement is not an empirical statement.

There are other, and important, ways in which it is not an empirical statement. Thus the claim that the limits of our language mean the limits of our world might be construed empirically in this way, by taking *language* narrowly, to refer to one's system of communication, its grammatical categories, etc., and *world* widely, to mean how in general the world appears to one, and the general framework of comprehension one applies to things; then, taking 'we' relatively to various linguistic groups, one would have the hypothesis, perhaps to be ascribed to Whorf, that the way things look to different groups profoundly depends on what their language is like. I shall come back to certain relativist questions raised by such theories. For the moment the aim is just the general one of illuminating by contrast the non-empirical character of an idealist interpretation of our slogan. If we are dealing with a genuinely empirical theory of this 'Whorfian' sort, then a given group's language should provide some sort of an empirical explanation, if only a very weak one, of its way of looking at the world. Connectedly, we could explain some particular person's way of looking at the world, or some aspect of that, by reference to the language group he or she belonged to. But all that cancels the force of the essentially first-personal, even though plural, formulation we are dealing with. An idealist interpretation will not be served by anything that merely puts any given 'we' in the world and then looks sideways at us. Under the idealist interpretation, it is not a question of our recognising that we are one lot in the world among others, and (in principle at least) coming to understand and explain how *our* language conditions *our* view of the world, while that of others conditions theirs differently. Rather, what the world is for us is shown by the fact that we can make sense of some things and not of others: or rather – to lose the last remnants of an empirical and third-personal view – in the fact that some things and not others make sense. Any empirical discovery we could make about our view of the world, as that it was conditioned by our use of count-words or whatever, would itself be a fact which we were able to understand in terms of, and only in terms of, our view of the world; and anything which radically we could not understand because it lay outside the boundary of our language would not be something we could come to explain our non-understanding of – it could not become clear to us what was wrong with it, or with us.

Here, in the contrast with a mere tautology and, very basically, in the contrast with an empirical view, we can begin to see an analogy between the plural view and the original first-person singular transcendental view. But still; why *idealism*? Enough reason, I think, is to be found in the considerations, rough as they are, which we have already put together, and which will serve also to tie those to certain identifiable concerns of the later Wittgenstein. Since the fact that our language is such and such, and thus that the world we live in is as it is, are, as presently construed, transcendental facts, they have no empirical explanation. Anything that can be empirically explained, as that certain external features of the world are this way rather than that, or that we (as opposed to the Hopi Indians, or again as opposed to cats) see things in a certain way, or deal with things in one way rather than another – all these fall *within* the world of our language, and are not the transcendental facts. In particular, in the sense in which we are now speaking of 'our language', there could be no explanation of it, or correlation of it with the world, in sociological terms, or zoological, or materialistic, in any of the several current senses of that expression. Indeed there could not be an explanation of it which was 'idealistic', in the *explanatory* sense of that term often used, e.g. by Marxist writers, of an explanation given in terms of conditioning ideas or thoughts, for there are no ideas or thoughts outside it to condition it. However, while we could not explain it in any of those ways, we could in a way make it clearer to ourselves, by reflecting on it, as it were self-consciously exercising it; not indeed by considering alternatives – for what I am presently considering can have no comprehensible alternatives to it – but by moving around reflectively inside our view of things and sensing when one began to be near the edge by the increasing incomprehensibility of things regarded from whatever way-out point of view one had moved into. What one would become conscious of, in so reflecting, is something like: *how we go on*. And *how we go on* is a matter of how we think, and speak, and intentionally and socially conduct ourselves: that is, matters of our experience.

As phenomenalism, regarded as a form of transcendental idealism, gave everything in terms of something mental, though in the only sense in which it could say that everything was mental, that statement was false; so *our* language, in this sense in which its being as it is has no empirical explanation, shows us everything as it appears to our interests, our concerns, our activities, though in the only sense in which we could meaningfully say that they determined everything, that statement would be false. The fact that in this way everything can be expressed only via human interests and concerns, things which are expressions of mind, and which themselves cannot ultimately be explained in any further terms: that provides grounds, I suggest, for calling such a view a kind of *idealism* (and not of the stupid 'aggregative' kind). The history of post-Kantian philosophy might in any case lead one to expect that there would be a place for such a view.

3 Relativism

We have here, in a vague sketch, the outline of a view. I have not yet offered any grounds for the claim that Wittgenstein held it. In fact, I am not going to claim anything as strong as that he held it. It seems to me that both the nature of the view, and the nature of the later Wittgenstein material, make it hard to substantiate any unqualified claim of that kind. I offer this model and its implied connection with the earlier work as a way of looking at and assessing that later material. But I will offer some considerations which suggest that the influence of the sort of view I have sketched is to be felt in the later work, and that reference to it may help to explain some curious and unsatisfactory features of that work. In particular it may help us to understand the use that Wittgenstein makes of 'we'. To reach any understanding on that matter, we have to approach it through the uninviting terrain of relativism.

In trying to distinguish a little while ago the transcendental version of 'the limits of our language mean the limits of our world' from an empirical version, I suggested one possible empirical version which I cavalierly labelled the Whorfian hypothesis, to the effect that language (narrowly construed) conditioned world-view (broadly construed). That was useful as an example (whether or not it represents the views of Whorf). It contains, we should now notice, three different elements. The first is that it takes language in a narrow sense, and the second is that it offers language in that sense as the explanation of the world-view. The third feature is that what are explained, or would be if there were a true such theory,[5] are various different world-views, held by different human sub-groups: there is more than one lot to call themselves 'we'. Now that of course follows from the first two points, since language in the narrow sense differs in the supposedly relevant respects between human groups. But, while still offering an empirical theory, one could drop the first point and keep the second and third: thus one would suppose that there were empirical explanations of differences in local world-view, but they did not lie in differences of language in the narrow sense.

Now as to the first point, I take it that Wittgenstein was not very interested, in these connections, in language in the narrow sense, and that he characteristically uses the term 'language' in a very extensive way, to embrace world-view rather than to stand in narrow and explanatory contradistinction to it. Hence his notoriously generous use of the expression 'language-game'; hence also, in the converse direction as it were, the tendency to use 'form of life' to refer to some quite modest linguistic practice. As Putnam[6] has justly said, '(the) fondness (of Wittgensteinians) for the expression "form of life" appears to be directly proportional to its degree of preposterousness in an given context'. The narrower sense of 'language' seems not to be an important factor in any explanations Wittgenstein would want to consider for variations of world-view between human groups. The question arises, then, of whether he is interested in any explanations at all.

---

[5] The references to the theory, like the references to Whorf, just function as a stand-in or dummy in the argument. I do not go into the difficulties that surround such a theory, such as that of independently characterising its explanandum.

[6] *Language, Belief and Metaphysics*, ed. Kiefer and Munitz (SUNY Press, 1970), p. 60.

I think in fact he is not basically interested in such explanations, and for a reason which I shall suggest ties up with our central question. Nevertheless at times he says things which would *prima facie* not rule out the possibility of explanation. At least, he thinks that a different way of looking at and talking about the world might become comprehensible in terms of different *interests*:

For here life would run on differently. – What interests us would not interest *them*. Here different concepts would no longer be unimaginable. In fact, this is the only way in which *essentially* different concepts are imaginable. (*Zettel*, 388)

Suggestions of a similar kind are to be found in the neighbourhood (378, 380), and in the preceding fragment a hint at a more specific kind of explanation might be detected (though hardly one which justifies what sounds like a tone of mild daring):

I want to say an education quite different from ours might also be the foundation for quite different concepts. (387)

In the work *On Certainty*, again, we have the recognition that a 'language-game' changes over time (256), and the model of the river (96 seq.), in which some hardened propositions can form the bank, which guides other more fluid propositions, but over time new bits may accumulate and old bits be swept away – this offers the *fact* of diachronic change, and it does not exclude, even if it does not encourage, the possibility of explaining such change. Thus both over time and over social space, variety and change are possible, and, so far as this goes, presumably we might have some explanations of that variety and change. Other ways of seeing the world are not imaginatively inaccessible to us; on the contrary, it is one of Wittgenstein's aims to encourage such imagination. We can consider alternatives, as in the examples I have already mentioned – and there are of course many more in which he suggests how people with different interests and concerns might describe, classify, and see the world differently from us. Thus the different world-pictures, as so far introduced, are not inaccessible to one another. Those who had one picture might come to see the point (in terms of interests, etc.) of another picture, and also perhaps come to understand why those who had it, did so. In that light, they could reflect also on their own world-picture, and understand, perhaps, something of why they had it. Thus in speaking of these various languages or world-pictures, it looks as though we are *not* speaking of things to which their subjects are, in terms of the idealism we have discussed, transcendentally related.

Now none of this yet implies anything about the *evaluative* comparability of different world-pictures. We have said that they are accessible to one another, to some extent, but that does not say anything, or anything much, about whether one could compare them with regard to adequacy. With regard, moreover, to those elements in the world-picture which purport to be truth-carrying, nothing has yet been determined about whether there is some objective basis from which one 'we' could come to recognise the greater truth of what was believed by another 'we'. But in fact, as is well known, Wittgenstein tends to say things which cast great doubt on that possibility, and not least in his last work. Thus *On Certainty* says (94):

I do not get my picture of the world [*Weltbild*] by satisfying myself of its correctness; nor do I have it because I am satisfied of its correctness. No: it is the inherited background against which I distinguish between true and false.

95. The propositions describing this world-picture might be part of a kind of mythology. And their role is like that of rules of a game; and the game can be learned purely practically, without learning any explicit rules.

And, revealingly, *On Certainty*, 298:

'We are quite sure of it' does not mean just that every single person is certain of it, but that we belong to a community which is bound together by science and education.

There are many remarks, again, which claim such things as that reasons can be given only within a game, and come to an end at the limits of the game (*Philosophische Grammatik*, p. 55), that our mode of representation is a language-game (*Philosophical Investigations*, p. 50), that 'grammar' cannot be justified (*Philosophische Bermerkungen*, p. 7), and that the language-game is not reasonable or unreasonable, but is there, like our life (*On Certainty*, 559). Nor is there any doubt that Wittgenstein included in the force of these remarks the kind of language-game which one human group might pursue and another lack. Thus in *On Certainty*, once more:

609. Suppose we met people who did not regard that (sc. the propositions of physics) as a telling reason. Now, how do we imagine this? Instead of the physicist, they consult an oracle. (And for that we consider them primitive.) Is it wrong for them to consult an oracle and be guided by it? – If

we call this 'wrong' aren't we using our language-game as a base from which to *combat* theirs?

610. And are we right or wrong to combat it? Of course there are all sorts of slogans which will be used to support our proceedings...

612. I said I would 'combat' the other man, – but wouldn't I give him *reasons*? Certainly; but how far do they go? At the end of reasons comes *persuasion*. (Think of what happens when missionaries convert natives.)

Now none of this, nor its negation, will follow from the idea just of different human groups empirically co-existing with different world-pictures which are (in the earlier, unambitious, sense) accessible to one another. Nor does it follow from a view or set of views which I have not so far mentioned, but which I shall come back to briefly at the end of these remarks, namely the view which has been charted by Dummett in much recent work, to the effect that *truth* must be replaced by, or interpreted in terms of, the notion of *conditions which justify assertion*. This view I shall summarily call Wittgenstein's constructivism. While constructivism must bring enquiry and speculation to a halt in what we have been trained to perceive as an adequate ground, this entails nothing about what different human groups may or may not have been trained to perceive as such a ground, nor about what they could be trained to perceive as a ground, nor about that they would find it natural to do when confronted with conflicts with what they think they already know. Constructivism might tell us something about *human* knowledge, not about that of narrower groups.

The relativist elements which have been added to this scene are extra, and do not follow from the rest. But once they are there, they have a curious and confusing effect backwards (so to speak) on the rest. For it will be remembered that one consideration that I used in characterising a transcendental interpretation of 'the limits of our language mean the limits of our world' was that the features of our language, so conceived, were not a matter of empirical explanation; and hence, conversely, that when we were dealing with what could be empirically explained, we had no such transcendentally isolated item. But if we add the relativist views, it looks as though the question, whether something is empirically explicable or not, is itself relative to a language; for such explanation, and *a fortiori*, particular forms of scientific explanation, are just some language-games among others. Thus our view of another world-picture, as something accessible, and empirically related, to ours, may just be a function of our world-picture; as, of course, may our supposed understanding of signs coming from the other group that they have the same feeling. Thus we lose hold at this level on the idea that they are *really* accessible. Once that alarm has broken out, we may indeed even begin to lose the hard-earned benefits of 'we' rather than 'I'. For if our supposed scientific understanding of the practices of other groups is to be seen merely as how those practices are *for us*, and if our experience of other forms of life is inescapably and non-trivially conditioned by our own form of life, then one might wonder what after all stops the solipsist doubt, that my experience which is supposedly of other individuals and the form of life which I share with them, cannot fail to be an experience only of how things are *for me*.

The point can be put also like this, that there is the gravest difficulty (familiar from certain positions in the philosophy of the social sciences) in both positing the independent existence of culturally distinct groups with different world-views, and also holding that any access we have to them is inescapably and non-trivially conditioned by our own world-view. For the very question from which we started, of the existence and relative accessibility of different world-views, becomes itself a function of one world-view. In fact what we have here is an exact analogue, at the social level, of aggregative solipsism.

So far as the social sciences are concerned, it is worth mentioning a certain view which is held by some followers of Wittgenstein, and which perhaps receives confused encouragement from the area we are considering. This is a view to the effect that it is possible to understand and at least piece-meal explain other outlooks, so long as the understanding is internalist and the explanation non-causal.[7] To suppose that that followed from general epistemological considerations at the level we are considering would be a muddle, representing something like aggregative solipsism (at the social level). For if relativist inaccessibility has taken over, then there are only two options: either one is submerged in, identical with an original member of, the other social system, in which case one has no explanations at all (except its own, if it happens to be self-conscious); or else one is necessarily bringing to it one's own conceptual outlook, in which case that will be no less so if what one is bringing is *Verstand* and Gestaltist redescription, than if one is bringing causal explanation. Of course,

[7] Itself, of course, an idealist view, in what I earlier called the 'explanatory' sense of the term.

there may be other good reasons for preferring the former type of explanation, but the project cannot just follow from some relativist story about the plurality of human language-games, as seems sometimes to be supposed.

The relativist elements introduce a persistent uncertainty in the interpretation of 'we', which not only makes the application of Wittgenstein's views unclear, but makes it unclear what kind of views they are. His references to conceptual change and to the different outlooks of different groups have a persistent vagueness which leaves it unclear how much room there is supposed to be for explanation. I earlier mentioned various cases in which Wittgenstein at least seemed to leave room for the possibility of explanation. But the range or determinacy of the explanations he left room for were, so far as the suggestions offered there went, exceedingly low – thus Wittgenstein referred sometimes in the weakest terms to what other people might find interesting, or related their practice in some broadly functional way to their interests. In some part, no doubt, these features of the work are owed to Wittgenstein's hatred of the cockiness of natural science, something which seems to me not easy in his case to distinguish from a hatred of natural science. His use of Gestaltist illumination can stun, rather than assist, further and more systematic explanation; to adapt a remark of Kreisel's,[8] when the child asks why the people on the other side of the world don't fall off, many would given an explanation in terms of gravity acting towards the centre of the earth, but Wittgenstein would draw a circle with a pin man on it, turn it round, and say, 'now *we* fall into space'.

Beyond that, however, the difficulties we have now run into raise the question of whether Wittgenstein is really thinking at all in terms of actual groups of human beings whose activities we might want to understand and explain. I think the answer to that is basically 'no'; we are not concerned so much with the epistemology of differing world-views, still less with the methodology of the social sciences, as with ways of exploring our world-view. We are concerned with the imagination, and the vaguely functionalist remarks we noticed before are not the sketch of an explanation, but an aid to the imagination, to make a different practice a more familiar idea to us, and hence to make us more conscious of the practice we have. Seen in this

[8] G. Kreisel, 'Wittgenstein's Theory and Practice of Philosophy', *British Journal for the Philosophy of Science*, xi (1960), pp. 238–52. Kreisel's own use of the point goes further than anything suggested here, and in a rather different direction.

light, the alternatives are not the sort of socially actual alternatives, relativistically inaccessible or not, which we have been discussing, nor are they offered as possible objects of any kind of explanation. Rather, the business of considering them is part of finding our way around inside our own view, feeling our way out to the points at which we begin to lose our hold on it (or it, its hold on us), and things begin to be hopelessly strange to us. The imagined alternatives are not alternatives *to* us; they are alternatives *for* us, markers of how far we might go and still remain, within our world – a world leaving which would not mean that we saw something different, but just that we ceased to see.

4   Non-relativist idealism

Relativism, then, is not really the issue. While the 'we' of Wittgenstein's remarks often looks like the 'we' of our group as contrasted with other human groups, that is basically misleading. Such a 'we' is not his prime concern, and even if one grants such views as the 'justified assertion' doctrine, the determination of meaning by social practice and so on, all of that leaves it open, how much humanity *shares* in the way of rational practice. Nor is it just a question of a final relativisation of 'we' to humanity. We cannot exclude the possibility of other language-using creatures whose picture of the world might be accessible to us. It must, once more, be an empirical question what degree of conceptual isolation is represented by what groups in the universe – groups *with* which we would be in the universe. If they are groups with which we are in the universe, and we can understand that fact (namely, that they are groups with a language, etc.), then they also *belong* to 'we'. Thus, while much is said by Wittgenstein about the meanings *we* understand being related to *our* practice, and so forth, that *we* turns out only superficially and sometimes to be one *we* as against others *in* the world, and thus the sort of *we* which has one practice as against others which are possible in the world. Leaving behind the confused and confusing language of relativism, one finds oneself with a *we* which is not one group rather than another in the world at all, but rather the plural descendant of that idealist *I* who also was not one item rather than another in the world.

But if that is the kind of *we* one is concerned with, it would, again, not follow (at least from this very general level of consideration) that any limit could be placed in advance on the scientific understanding of human practice and human meanings. For if we empirically differ from other groups in the universe with regard to the world-picture we have, then it might be possible to find an explanation of that difference, in terms of our differing evolution, our situation in different environments in the universe, or whatever. But if we could do that for ourselves (that is, humanity) if there turned out to be others to compare ourselves with, then it could not be impossible, though it might be harder, to do it for ourselves without our knowing of others, or without there being others. Even if we, humanity, were the only lot in the world, a transcendental idealism of the first-person plural could not rule out in itself the possibility of an empirical or scientific understanding of why, as persons who have evolved in a particular way on a particular planet, we have the kind of world-picture we have – even though such an explanation would, once more, have to lie within the limits of our language, in the only sense of 'our' in which they would mean the limits of our world. But if all that is possible, there is little left of the thought that those limits are *limits* at all: it might turn out with this sort of idealism, too, that 'when its implications are followed out strictly, it coincides with pure realism'.

Yet when that was so in the *Tractatus* case, the work itself, notoriously and professedly, tried nevertheless to go beyond it. I will end by suggesting that the later work may be seen also as trying to do that, or rather not preventing itself from doing that, with its own elements of a pluralised idealism. This concerns what I earlier called the 'constructivism'. This has many roots, particularly in the theory of knowledge, which I shall not try to say anything about. But a central thought it contains is one that can be put by saying that our sentences have the meaning we give them, and from that some important consequences are supposed to follow, with regard to their logic not being able to determine reality beyond, so to speak, what was put into it in the first place. Relatedly, the notion of 'truth' is to be replaced by, or interpreted in terms of, an appeal to the conditions which have been determined to be appropriate for the assertion of a given sensence.[9] But it is not easy to see, at least at first, how if this set of views is not a triviality, which has no important consequences at all, it can avoid having quite amazing consequences. For consider the

---

[9] See M. Dummett, 'Wittgenstein's Philosophy of Mathematics', *Phil. Rev.* (1959), reprinted in his *Truth and Other Enigmas* (London: Duckworth, 1978).

following argument-schema, which I have discussed in a slightly different form elsewhere:[10]

(i) '*S*' has the meaning we give it.

(ii) A necessary condition of our giving '*S*' a meaning is Q.

ergo (iii) Unless Q, '*S*' would not have a meaning.

(iv) If '*S*' did not have a meaning, '*S*' would not be true.

ergo (v) Unless Q, '*S*' would not be true.

It looks as though there should be something wrong with this argument, since any number of substitutions for Q in (ii) which relate to human existence, language use, etc., make it true for any '*S*' one likes, and since (i) is supposedly true for any '*S*', and (iv) for any true '*S*', we can get the truth of any true '*S*' dependent on human existence etc.; that is, prove unrestricted idealism. Now on some traditional views, there is no need to find anything wrong with the argument in order to avoid this, since (i) will be taken to be true just in case "'*S*'" names a sentence, and in that case (v) can be harmlessly true, as meaning "Unless Q, '*S*' would not express a truth", and that of course will not entail: Unless Q, not S. But it is not obvious that for later Wittgensteinian views, and in particular for the theory of justified assertion, we can so easily drive a line between the sentence '*S*' expressing the truth, and what is the case if S. Wittgenstein does indeed sometimes speak in these connections as though he were talking simply about the sentences of natural languages, and produces some very odd results, as at *PI*, I, 381:

How do I know that this colour is red? – It would be an answer to say: 'I have learnt English'.

which is a translation of

Wie erkenne ich, daß diese Farbe Rot ist? – Eine Antwort wäre: 'Ich habe Deutsch gelernt'.

But at least that is a case of someone's *knowing* something, and the difficulties, though revealing, are comparatively superficial. But if we are considering what would be true if..., and if we are to replace the notion of truth-conditions with that of assertion-conditions, and if we are to grant, what Wittgenstein surely holds, that for anything to have come to be an assertion-condition for a given sentence involves certainly a human practice, and perhaps a human decision; then

---

[10] 'Knowledge and Meaning in the Philosophy of Mind', *Phil. Rev.*, lxxv (1966), reprinted in *Problems of the Self* (Cambridge, 1973).

something has to be done if we are to avoid even empirical idealism. The obvious thing to do is to regard talk about what would be the case if there were no human beings, language, etc., as talk about what *would* justify the assertion of certain sentences which we do understand (of which the assertion-conditions are fixed). That banishes the empirical idealism, since it removes any reference to convention-fixing from the hypothetical unpopulated scene, nor does it record any piece of convention-fixing. But it would give reason to reflect that any given supposition is determinate only because, on the theory, there is at some point a decision to count certain conditions as adequate for assertion. That reflection is more radical, and is meant to be more radical, than the banal thought in standing back from a sentence describing a non-human event, that if there were no human events there would be no such sentence. The point comes out rather in the thought that the determinacy of reality comes from what we have decided or are prepared to count as determinate:

We have a colour system as we have a number system. Do the systems reside in *our* nature or in the nature of things? How are we to put it? – *Not* in the nature of things. (*Zettel*, 357)

The diffidence about how to put it comes once more from a problem familiar in the *Tractatus*: how to put a supposed philosophical truth which, if it is uttered, must be taken to mean an empirical falsehood, or worse. For of course, if our talk about the numbers has been determined by our decisions, then one result of our decisions is that it must be nonsense to say that anything about a number has been determined by our decisions. The dependence of mathematics on our decisions, in the only sense in which it obtains – for clearly there cannot be meant an empirical dependence on historical decisions – is something which shows itself in what we are and are not prepared to regard as sense and is not to be stated in remarks about decisions; and similarly in other cases. The new theory of meaning, like the old, points in the direction of a transcendental idealism, and shares also the problem of our being driven to state it in forms which are required to be understood, if at all, in the wrong way.

13   Another time, another place, another person

In *Language, Truth and Logic* Ayer proceeded on the basis that a sentence uttered by *A* on a given occasion, if it was to have empirical meaning, had to make a statement which was verifiable by *A* on that occasion, and this led to the well known reduction of statements about the past to statements about present evidence, and of third-personal statements about the mental to statements about observable behaviour. (Statements about the future, of course, are not strictly speaking verifiable at the time of utterance, but nevertheless were allowed to count, presumably because there is something that the utterer can start to do at the time of utterance which will, in principle, issue in verification – roughly, waiting and seeing.)

Later[1] he moved to the position of saying that there is no class of statements which are statements about the past or about other minds, just as there is no class of statements which are statements about elsewhere. One and the same statement is made by one who speaks of a given event from a future, a present or a past perspective. An utterance using token-reflexive devices can be seen as doing two things at once: 'by combining a description of the event in question with a reference to the temporal position of the speaker, the use of tenses brings together two pieces of information which are logically distinct'.[2] This doctrine he employed to reject the reductionist views of *Language, Truth and Logic*: 'propositions about the past are not about the present or future: they are about the past', he rather misleadingly put it at

---

[1] Principally in 'Statements about the Past' and 'One's Knowledge of Other Minds', reprinted in A. J. Ayer, *Philosophical Essays* (London: Macmillan, 1954); and in A. J. Ayer, *The Problem of Knowledge* (London: Macmillan, 1956; Harmondsworth: Penguin, 1956). Because of the kind of points I want to discuss, I have concentrated on Ayer's work of this period, ten to twenty years after *Language, Truth and Logic*, 1st edn (London: Gollancz, 1936). There is no suggestion that these were Ayer's final views on these subjects.

[2] Ayer, *Problem*, Penguin edn, p. 180.

one point,[3] meaning by that not the denial of what he had just asserted, but that such propositions are about the events they seem to be about, and not about some other and later events.

The theory starts, then, with *token sentences* (type sentences used on a given occasion by a given speaker), and uses, in effect, the notion of a *convergent* set of such sentences – where a set of token sentences is convergent if[4] all its members have, with regard to reference secured by token-reflexive devices, the same reference, and otherwise are synonymous. (A convergent set of token sentences can be regarded as having as members more than actually uttered sentences: we can identify type sentences, occasions and speakers, such that token sentences determined by these items can be conceived and assigned to a set, though not actually uttered – and no doubt type sentence and occasion alone may serve to locate a merely possible speaker as well.) The members of what I am calling a convergent set of token sentences are said by Ayer to have the same factual content[5] and to convey the same information (apart from the information about the speaker s perspective),[6] and he is prepared to say that in a way they have the same meaning,[7] though this is subject to the obvious reservation that there is an everyday application of 'meaning' under which members of a convergent set can have different meanings, as '$S(\ldots I \ldots)$' would naturally be said to have a different meaning from '$S(\ldots he \ldots)$' even when the first is said by A and the second is said by someone of A.

As we have seen, Ayer is disposed to see each member of the convergent set as both offering a common-core statement or proposition – in the simplest case, asserting it – and as revealing at the same time the perspective from which the proposition, is, in each case, offered. In fact, he goes beyond this[8] in supposing, further, that it must be possible to represent the core proposition in its own right, so to speak, in the form of what I shall call a *neutral sentence*. Since a neutral sentence presents the proposition to which token-reflexive devices express particular approaches, it is itself free from all token-reflexive

---

[3] Ayer, 'One's Knowledge', in *Philosophical Essays*, p. 201.
[4] Only a sufficient condition is offered; there is no need here to involve ourselves in the general problems of statement identity, in particular with regard to reference secured by expressions other than token reflexives.
[5] Ayer, 'Statements', in *Philosophical Essays*, p. 186; cf. Ayer, *Problem*, pp. 179, 180.
[6] Ayer, 'Statements', in *Philosophical Essays*, p. 187.
[7] Ibid., p. 186; cf. Ayer, *Problem*, Penguin edn, pp. 180–1.
[8] That there is a further step here is brought out by Michael Dummett in his *Frege: Philosophy of Language* (London: Duckworth, 1973).

devices. With respect to time, the neutral sentence is what Quine calls an eternal sentence, a sentence which cannot change its truth value. Hence, on Ayer's theory, there lies behind the apparatus of token-reflexive speech a representation of the world *sub specie aeternitatis*, a representation of it as seen from no point of view (time, place, person) rather than any other, and the neutral sentences form this representation.

It is important to stress the point that this goes beyond the mere requirements of statement identity. We could understand the idea of a convergent set, and assign token sentences to such sets, without supposing that there could be a neutral sentence which represented their common eternal, impersonal, and so on, content. A consequence of this stronger view is that, if there is a sense in which all the members of a convergent set have the same meaning, then the neutral sentence at their core gives the meaning which they all have – a claim which seems less inviting than the claim, merely, that there is a sense in which they all have the same meaning. If we stick to their having the same 'factual content', however, it seems more acceptable to say that the members of the convergent set, and the core neutral sentence, share the same factual content. For one thing, there seems room for the idea that theoretical material might occur in characterising the factual content of both the neutral sentence and the everyday token–reflexive sentences which constitute the convergent set. (The question of theoretical material in the neutral sentence is one I shall touch on later.)

Ayer seems, in fact, to have made a further demand on the neutral sentence: that its non-logical vocabulary should consist only of descriptions, and should eliminate not only the token–reflexive expressions which it is required *ex hypothesi* to eliminate, but also all proper names. It may be, indeed, that Ayer has regarded this not as a further demand, but as following from the identity of factual content. He expresses a related idea in terms of the notion of descriptive adequacy: 'since what can be described in a language depends only on what predicates it contains, replacing indicators by predicates can never impoverish a language descriptively'.[9] The general doctrine, and any reasons there may be for it, need not concern us here, but there is a particular application of it, with regard to persons, which we shall encounter a little later.

---

[9] A. J. Ayer, 'Individuals', repr. in *Philosophical Essays*, p. 21. The 'since' presumably introduces an inference, but I confess I find it hard to find an inference here which is not either question-begging or invalid.

There is one further point to be made about this apparatus, concerning the interpretation of token reflexives. I am taking 'token-reflexive' fairly broadly, in a sense in which 'now' is token-reflexive just because it is a rule of its meaning that, if you are to know what time is in question on an occasion of its utterance, you have to know when it is uttered. Ayer takes the token-reflexivity of 'now' in the strict sense that the token-reflexive reference is to be explained in terms of the token utterance, so that 'now' is actually explicated as 'at the same time as this utterance', and 'past', consequently, comes out as meaning 'earlier than this utterance'. But (even leaving aside Prior's well known difficulty of the content, on this account, of 'Thank God that's over') it is very doubtful that as an explication this will possibly do. Surely it is only in virtue of having already grasped 'now' that you can be led to the very special, variable application of 'this utterance' which is needed for this account. But this is a side issue in relation to the construction of convergent sets as such; it is a separate issue which token-reflexive expressions, and how many, are primitive.

We may now turn to the question of the verification of the neutral sentence. Let a given neutral sentence S state the occurrence of an event E as occurring at place P at time T. It is assumed that there is an optimal verification point (OVP) for S. It is further assumed that this point is the space–time position (P, T). We shall accept the first assumption, leaving the possibility open, however, that the OVP for given S need not be unique. The second assumption, however, raises doubts. It is common ground, of course, that P and T will not be independently optimal: thus the time of verification T may be the best time only if one is at P, and the place of verification P the best place only if one is there at T. But, apart from that, relative to what order of assumptions is the combination (P, T) optimal for the verification of S – that is to say, the observation (if S is true) of E? It may be said that it is a necessary truth that (P, T) is the origin of information about the event E, and that in principle information must decay between (P, T) and any other at least moderately distant point. But this raises the question of what level of principle gives this result, and relative to what methods of verification or observation the 'information' – as genuinely knowledge-giving information – may be thought to decay. It might be thought that it was relative to some deep laws of nature that information decayed away from the origin; but then equally it could be relative to no less deep laws of nature that the event point was, for instance, not a possible point of observation at all, such as that which cosmologists call the first few seconds of the universe. Certainly this is not a question which can just be disposed of with a distinction between 'in practice' and 'in principle', like the old difficulty for phenomenalism about the hypothetical observer in whose presence Crippen would not have murdered his wife.[10]

It is hard to see in fact how the notion of an OVP (for a given kind of event, and hence − surely − for a given kind of observation) can be freed from empirical, or at any rate non-logical, considerations. But, if that is right, then some part of the traditional sceptical problem which has worried Ayer seems to evaporate. One thing that worries the sceptic, as Ayer represents him, is that, short of full-blown verification, grounds for merely probable or reasonable belief in the event cannot be found at all. But if the notion of full-blown verification implies the notion of an OVP, and the notion of an OVP, or rather the use of that notion in any given concrete kind of case, involves the kind of consideration just mentioned, that set of considerations might equally be expected to yield the idea of points other than the OVP from which observations might be gained − giving less than full-blown verification but leading to reasonable belief. The understanding, which is needed to set up the problem, that certain positions are disadvantaged relative to the OVP, could yield an understanding of why and how they are disadvantaged − and that is something which can give a backing to probable belief.

The treatment of scepticism is not my concern, but the present point has a wider application. It leads, in fact, to one paradox of positivism. For positivism, meaning has to be given in terms of verification, and meaning has to be prior to fact. Verification, moreover, has to be explicated, especially for positivism, in terms of observation. But what we understand about observation and its relations to different kinds of event is not totally prior to fact. We are left with unclear empirical assumptions in the concept of verification.

It is not easy to judge the extent of the purely necessary dimensions of the notion of an OVP. Relative to the propositions that causes precede effects and that all information is an effect, it is necessary that the present time does not contain the OVP for a sentence about an event which lies in the future. It is rather less obvious, relative to those assumptions, that the same is true with respect to all sentences about events which lie in the past. Other problems arise about what is happening elsewhere. It is not clear, moreover, to what extent the

[10] A. J. Ayer, 'Phenomenalism', reprinted in *Philosophical Essays*, pp. 151–2.

absolutely pure conception of verification is entitled to those assumptions themselves.

We shall leave these points, however, and consider what follows when we have identified some non-optimal verification points for a given event – allowing that, for many kinds of event, at least, being in the past or elsewhere relative to a given observer puts it away from the OVP for that observer. Ayer has worried a good deal about the conditions under which such an event could nevertheless be said to be verifiable by me, if I am that observer – where 'verifiable by me' means 'might in principle have been verified by me'. Thus, what is now happening elsewhere from where I am cannot, as things are, be (optimally) verified by me, since if I am at P_j at T_k, then necessarily I am not at $P_i (i \neq j)$ at T_k, nor is there anything I can now do to bring it about that I am there at just that time. But this is only a relative necessity. It is not necessary that I am at P_j at T_k, and in particular I might have been at P_i at T_k. This satisfies the demand for verifiability in principle by me.

A different application of what at first looks like the same thing occurs with the past. If E_i occurred at T_i (T_i earlier than T_k) then there is nothing I can do at T_k to bring it about that at T_k or later I optimally verify E_i. But I might have optimally verified it. It is even conceivable, perhaps, that I might have existed much earlier than I actually exist, so that it is conceivable that I might have verified events which occurred long before my actual birth-date.[11] This last idea involves of course a contrary-to-fact possibility, as did the issue of the verifiability in principle of what is elsewhere. But it is notable that, in the case of the past of my own lifetime, the possibility of having verified the event directly is not necessarily contrary to fact. Perhaps I actually did observe the event in question.

This consideration raises a problem about this whole set of procedures. Do these questions about what I can conceive as verifiable by me involve in any way my knowledge? The point, mentioned by Ayer, that there is an increasing difficulty in my conceiving my displacement to more remote times may imply that the thought experiment is to be regarded as one for me, and bounded by my knowledge of my own lifetime and circumstances. But relative to that perspective, no question about the verifiability in principle by me of my own remembered past seems to arise – I just did verify the propositions in question. I conceive myself in terms to which memory has already been given, before I embark on thought experiments about what may or may not be verifiable by me.

If, on the other hand, the question of verifiability by me can be considered from a purely neutral point of view, as an instance of verifiability by X, then it is quite unclear why conceivable verifiability by *me* is an issue at all, and not just a misplaced hangover from earlier views in the context of the 'neutral sentences' theory. Regarded from the outside, from the neutral point of view, it is of no interest at all for these problems whether an individual who actually exists at T_k, me, could in principle be extended or displaced temporally backwards to a time T_i earlier than T_k, so as to encounter an event E_i conceived from the neutral point of view as occurring then. If the neutral point of view is comprehensible to us at all, then the very most that could count from that point of view, surely, is that someone could directly verify E_i at T_i, and the whole issue of whether that person might conceivably have been me totally falls out of the question.

An ambivalence related to this is displayed in some of Ayer's arguments about other minds. Here he thinks that we have at least the same relative impossibility as with space: if I am the person with characteristics C, and you are the person with contrary characteristics C', then necessarily I am not you. Indeed, in a sense, under all circumstances I am necessarily not you, since 'I' and 'you' are deployed only by and with regard to persons characterised severally by such characteristics. However, it seems not to follow that I could not have had C': 'so long as I do not limit the possibilities by forming a picture of myself with which anything that I imagine has to be reconciled, I can conceive of having any consistent set of characteristics that you please. All that is required is that the possession of the characteristics be something that is in itself empirically verifiable.'[12] Earlier Ayer had thought that there might be some limits to what was conceivable in this direction, some properties being taken as constitutive of oneself; but this limit could be lightly lifted, since the question of what was constitutive of oneself was itself conventional, arbitrary, and to be decided on the spot.[13]

I shall not discuss the issue of how the notion of an OVP applies

[12] Ibid., p. 249.

[13] Ayer, 'One's Knowledge', in *Philosophical Essays*, pp. 211–12: 'whether it is conceivable that I should satisfy some description which I actually do not...will depend on what properties I choose, for the occasion, to regard as constitutive of myself...it is contradictory only if one chooses to make it so'.

at all to the question of psychological states, nor whether Ayer is right in using the familiar model that one who is in pain is in the best position for verifying that he is in pain. Using that model, Ayer conceives verifiability in principle by me as the possibility that I might conceivably have satisfied the descriptions C' which actually characterise you, and in those circumstances would or would not have found myself (so to speak) in pain. Now it is extremely unclear that Ayer has the right at all on his views of token reflexives and the descriptive eliminability of indicator words to describe this situation as that of *my* satisfying C' – any more than the conceivable situation of my being at P_i rather than, as I am, at P_j would be a situation of P_i being here. Rather, under Ayer's assumptions, the situation emerges as that of your existing and my not doing so. At the very least, it cannot make the slightest difference which way the situation is described, on those assumptions: the 'factual content' will be the same, there will be no 'descriptive difference'. Then verifiability by me finally drops out: verifiability is the most that can be left.

This is just a special application of what has already been emerging: that there is a very poor fit between, on the one hand, the matter of verification by me, which in the form of *conceivable* verification by me, continued to preoccupy Ayer, and on the other hand, the *sub specie aeternitatis* view of the world, with its descriptive content embodied in neutral sentences. This is a second paradox of positivism. The empiricist element pulls back to the egocentric predicament, while the respect for the physicist's world-view leads to the eternal or neutral conception of the world. Ayer sees the neutral-sentences model as the correct model for science and equally as a representation of the world as it is in itself, as opposed to the various perspectives we have on it. This honours the commitments of positivism as *wissenschaftliche Weltauffassung*. But the role of verifiability by me, even of conceivable verifiability by me, in relation to this model is incurably anomalous. In grasping the neutral model, I already have the idea of a world of events, some of which, from my particular location inside it, I may conceivably verify or have verified, others not.

The issue, then, can at most be verifiability *by someone*. But difficult questions remain about what force can be given even to that in the context of the neutral-sentences view and, more generally, in the context of a philosophy which tries to represent adequately a scientific view of the world. These difficulties present themselves differently depending on what motivation is assumed for the demand for verifiability. I believe that some version of them will always emerge under any verificationist assumptions, but I shall confine myself here to a kind of difficulty which arises specifically from the sort of interest that Ayer has had in verifiability.

For Ayer, the motivation towards verificationism lay in the epistemological concerns of empiricism. Verification was seen in terms of observation, and observation in terms of perception, and it was this consideration that underlay the approach to meaning. Even after the demands of the strongest reductive verficationism had been relaxed, the meaning of empirical sentences was to be controlled by what they could mean for us in terms of our experience. But, from the perspective of the neutral model, the question must arise of the respects in which our experience may itself be misleading or partial.

At a particular level, the neutral-sentences model admits this fact: any person's actual situation will be remote from the OVP for various events. Moreover, the model, or rather the philosophical explanations that go with it, even provide one quite pervasive sense in which our experience is misleading. It is metaphysically misleading, since it naturally presents the world to us as being other than as it is correctly displayed in the neutral-sentences model. But these considerations do not take us far enough. In the neutral-sentences model, all disadvantages of an observation point tend to be assimilated to the disadvantages of location: if one is not at the OVP, one is *elsewhere*. This emerges in the problems about temporal displacement we have already considered. It applies, in a way, to the problem of other minds: the observer is pictured, even if obscurely, as not being at the site of the psychological action. Earlier, I suggested that there was an empirical element in the notion of an OVP at all, and that question arises even when the idea of a better or worse observation point is considered, in this way, solely in terms of displacement. But it is far more so when the inquiry is extended, as it should be, beyond the displacement picture to the matter of the general quality or character of our perceptual experience. It is then a question not just of being at the right place at the right time, but of what happens to one when one is.

Scientific understanding can be expected to yield a critique of experience in the light of theory, and certain general aspects of our experience will be seen from that to be strongly influenced by our make-up. This goes importantly beyond the particular disadvantages of particular locations. The neutral-sentences model tries to view all events from the outside, from no particular point of view, but it will remain crucially flawed if it does not address itself to the question of the terms in which the events which form the contents of the model are to be characterised, how theoretical the characterisation of them should be, and how far it must abstract from peculiarities of the human perception of the world. The objective of giving a representation of the world which is not a representation from here or from any other particular perspective will not have been achieved, even after abstraction from time and place, if the terms in which the representation is given are peculiarly our perceptual terms – or, peculiarly, anyone else's. That would be only another perspectival distortion. The aim of overcoming that distortion could not in principle be achieved by verificationist empiricism, and this provides a reason why (even when verifiability by me is no longer the issue) its relation to the neutral-sentences model must be incoherent.

Verificationism of this kind must be incoherent in relation not just to the neutral-sentences model, but to any view which seeks to offer what may be called an 'absolute' representation of the world, in the sense (ambitious enough, but less ambitious than some other senses that have been given to the expression) of a representation of the world as it is, as opposed to how it peculiarly appears to any group in virtue of that group's peculiarities.[14] Some will doubt that any such absolute picture of the world can be achieved, and in particular that it can be achieved by scientific inquiry. But those who have hoped for a philosophy centred on the scientific world-view have not doubted this, but have rather based their philosophy on a hopeful vision of a scientific picture of the world just because they thought, and with reason, that such a picture was the only thing that could achieve an absolute representation of things. It has been thought, and certainly thought by positivists, that the positivist attachment to verifiability was connected with its objective of being a philosophy of the scientific world-view. But, if the present line of argument is right, the verificationist bias of positivism constituted, on the contrary, a basic obstacle to its being such a philosophy.

[14] I have tried to say some more about this conception, its history and its present situation, in *Descartes: The Project of Pure Enquiry* (Harmondsworth: Penguin, 1978).